Grandparent's Guide to Autism Spectrum Disorders

Grandparent's Guide to Autism Spectrum Disorders

Making the Most of the Time at Nana's House

Nancy Mucklow

6448 Vista Dr.
Shawnee, KS 66218
www.aapcpublishing.net

©2012 AAPC Publishing
6448 Vista Dr.
Shawnee, KS 66218
www.aapcpublishing.net

Publisher's Cataloging-in-Publication

Mucklow, Nancy.

Grandparent's guide to autism spectrum disorders : making the most of the time at Nana's house / Nancy Mucklow. -- Shawnee Mission, Kan. : AAPC Publishing, c2012.

p. ; cm.
ISBN: 978-1-937473-06-8
LCCN: 2012942653
Includes bibliographical references.
Summary: Helpful guide to prepare grandparents for the special needs and unique talents of children with autism spectrum disorders.--Publisher.
Contents: What is an autism spectrum disorder? -- Too hot, too cold: being sensitive about sensory issues -- The perfect storm: dealing with emotional issues -- Social situations: becoming a seeing-eye dog -- Self-regulation: focusing the executive function -- Grandma's house, Grandma's rules: controlling behavior -- Simple language: bridging communication barriers -- Education: learning beyond school -- Matriarch, patriarch: leading the family into acceptance -- Conclusion -- References -- Recommended resources.

1. Autism in children. 2. Grandparents of children with disabilities--Handbooks, manuals, etc. 3. Autistic children--Care. 4. Children with autism spectrum disorders--Care. 5. Autistic children--Family relationships. 6. Children with autism spectrum disorders--Family relationships. I. Title.

RJ506.A9 M83 2012
618.92/85882--dc23   1208

This book is designed in Myriad Pro.
Cover Art: iStockphoto © Kateryna Davydenko
Printed in the United States of America.

Table of Contents

Introduction

Lesia was three years old when her pediatrician told her parents that she had an autism spectrum disorder. They were overwhelmed but soon just rolled up their sleeves and rearranged their lives around the child.

Lesia's maternal grandparents, May and Wilfred, watched with some concern. "Nothing wrong with that kid," Wilf would often say, especially when Lesia was visiting. "She needs a firm hand, that's all." But May noticed that Wilf rarely spent any time with the child, choosing to do yardwork when Lesia came for visits.

So Lesia became largely May's responsibility during visits. May found her impossible to control. Lesia wouldn't listen or obey. May tried to set rules for her house and be a sensible grandparent, but the tantrums, screaming, and fixations drove her crazy. Everything she tried to get Lesia's behavior under control only seemed to make it worse.

May loved her grandchild and wanted to be as supportive as possible to her daughter and son-in-law, but the truth was – she was a little bit afraid to have Lesia around.

Meanwhile, May noticed that Lesia's other grandparents, Lucia and Leo, let Lesia run pretty much wild. They showered her with gifts and attention. They ignored the misbehavior and the meltdowns and didn't seem to mind that Lesia's antics drew a lot of attention in public. Their attitude was that all children grow up eventually.

Yet, May couldn't help but notice that Lucia and Leo rarely took Lesia for more than a couple of hours on a weekend.

Grandparents are important in the life of any child. Any grandparent will tell you: It goes both ways. A special connection with your grandchildren is a joy.

But when a grandchild has an autism spectrum disorder (ASD),[1] the relationship can be a bit daunting.

What do I do when I'm with him? How will I know how to handle difficult situations such as meltdowns and tantrums? What can we do together if she doesn't like anything? Will I make her behavior worse?

It's important to acknowledge the challenges of being an involved and loving grandparent when the child has an ASD. It's not easy. Typical children fit into Grandma's house instinctively – obeying, trying to please, finding their groove. With children with ASD, even a brief visit can leave you mentally and physically exhausted. Typical children give lots of rewards – through smiles, chatter, and shared fun. With children with ASD, those rewards can be rare and hard won.

Nobody wants to leave one grandchild out. So it's important to get a handle on grandparenting the child with ASD. With a little bit of information and a few tips that work, you'll learn to be a vital part of your grandchild's life and enjoy the experience.

---

1 Autism spectrum disorder is a broad term to describe pervasive development disorders such as autism, Asperger Syndrome, childhood disintegrative disorder, Rett Syndrome, and pervasive development disorder-not otherwise specified (PDD-NOS). Please note some of this terminology may change in 2013. See page 11.

Emotions

When your grandchild was diagnosed, a flurry of attention focused on the feelings and needs of the parents and the child. There's nothing wrong with that. But now it's time to acknowledge that *you* as a grandparent have feelings, too.

Many grandparents report conflicting feelings on hearing the diagnosis – concern, confusion, sadness, disbelief, resentment, and relief. You can be sure the child's parents are feeling those emotions as well. But the sooner everyone rolls up their sleeves and gets informed and involved, the sooner things get better.

- **Confusion:** ASD isn't something you're familiar with. The child's parents are getting a lot of information and experience, so they seem to know what they're doing, but you feel as if you're in over your head.

- **Hesitation:** You don't want to interfere or do anything wrong. You believe it's best to let the parents handle everything.

- **Reluctance:** If you've witnessed one of your grandchild's meltdowns, especially in public, you may have a knot in your stomach at the mere thought of experiencing it again.

- **Sadness:** You may be mourning the loss of your dream of a perfect grandchild. You may also be wondering if a relationship with him is even possible.

- **Guilt:** You can end up feeling guilty for having any of these emotions. You may also feel guilty because you think that you should be doing more, even though you know you need to live your own life.

The goal of this book is to replace these feelings with new feelings that will contribute to a happier relationship:

- **Acceptance:** You'll know the basics of ASD and recognize how it's part of your grandchild's personality and whole being. You'll gain new respect for his talents and personal strengths.

- **Confidence:** You'll understand how your grandchild experiences the world, and you'll have tips and ideas to try to support him.

- **Realistic expectations:** You'll abandon any dreams of making your grandchild more "normal." Instead, you'll dream new dreams that are based on who she is.

How to respond to friends who say, "He looks normal to me."

We live in a culture obsessed with "normal." When friends make comments that imply that ASD is nothing to deal with, avoid the temptation to launch into a speech. They don't need the details, and you don't need to explain. Just turn it into a compliment: *"Thank you. He's working really hard at it. I'll let him know you think he's doing a great job."*

Different Types of Grandparents

Grandparents have different levels of involvement. Some can spend less time, some more time, with their grandchildren. Your grandchild doesn't need perfect grandparents; he needs loving grandparents. The point is to give your grandchild what he needs.

- **Traditional Grandparents:** If you're a traditional grandparent, you believe that the parents must make all decisions about their child. You don't want to interfere. You like to visit and bring presents, and tend to be formal. This may not sound like the description of an "ideal" grandparent, but since children with ASD like routines and sameness, they're very comfortable with traditional grandparents.

- **Spare-Parent Grandparents:** If you're a spare-parent grandparent, you live nearby and are very involved in the family's life. You help as much as you can, but you're aware that you need to take the time to have your own life, too.

- **Embedded Grandparents:** If you're an embedded grandparent, you live with the extended family under the same roof. You're like a third parent, involved in the decisions. There may be lots of demands on your time. On the other hand, you may have shaped your life so that you have as much freedom as you need.

- **Fun Grandparent:** If you're a fun grandparent, you're active and like to play. You seek time with your grandchildren so that you can enjoy their liveliness. Authority and rules seem less important to you. This can work out fine, as long as there's enough routine and accommodations for the child.

- **Distance Grandparents:** If you're a distance grandparent, you live far away and visit once or twice a year. You may be geographically distant, but that doesn't mean you have to be emotionally distant. In our electronic age, there are many ways to stay connected all the time.

- **Primary-Care Grandparents:** If you're a primary-care grandparent, you're actively raising your grandchild. If you're the one with full or partial custody, make sure you take advantage of all the help and support available. Raising a child with ASD can be exhausting. Your school, healthcare network, and local autism center or group can direct you to your local services. Find books on parenting a child with ASD so that you know as much as parents do. Get as involved as possible in the child's education. But remember that you'll need respite, too. Many autism centers can help arrange respite care. If that isn't possible, consider paying an adult babysitter so you can get away once in a while.

Support Groups

Grandparent support groups aren't as common as parent support groups, but they're out there. Contact your community information center or senior center to find out what kinds of grandparent groups are available. You may also be able to find them on the Internet by searching your city's name combined with "Grandparents Raising Grandchildren," "Parenting Again," "Grandparent Support Group," or "Grandparents Association." Your local autism center or organization may be aware of groups specifically for grandparents of children on the autism spectrum. In addition, social networking websites often have support groups for grandparents of children with ASD.

If you can't find a group, your local senior center may be a place to find other grandparents of children with ASD. Having someone to talk to who understands your situation will help you deal better with your grandchild.

What Grandparents Offer to the Grandchild With ASD

- **Grandparents can fill out the family.** Grandparents, aunts, uncles, and other family members are often involved in helping to raise children with ASD. Some grandparents live far away and can't be around as much as they'd like to, whereas others live in the extended family household and are part of the child's day-to-day life. The amount of involvement varies, but grandparents often have a special place in kids' hearts.

- **Grandparents have a lifetime of experience to share.** Even though they may not know much about ASD, at least at first, grandparents know a lot about life. They know that if a strategy fails the first time, it just might work the second time. They look at the big picture and have a long-term perspective. This helps them relax and enjoy their time with the grandchild.

- **Grandparents have time.** Many grandparents are retired or near-retired, so they are able to spend long stretches of time with their grandchildren. They often also have patience. Parents are often harried, rushing to fit everything into their schedule while working and keeping the house going. Grandparents usually don't have the same pressures.

- **Grandparents don't care so much what other people think.** They're often more accepting and less embarrassed by meltdowns in public and behaviors that other people would consider odd.

The Future

Autism spectrum disorders are something to accept, adapt to, and even celebrate. Many gifted scientists, artists, musicians, and actors have an ASD, and some of the most pivotal people in history are thought to have had an ASD. They're people who are different, outliers who see the world through different eyes. What's more, they're capable of original thought. That means they can come up with new solutions to the world's problems and point us in new directions.

You can help pave the way with loving support, happy childhood memories, and a warm hand to hold.

Chapter 1

What Is an Autism Spectrum Disorder?

Ling watched her six-year-old grandson Tim playing by himself with his trains, lining them up over and over again. She was trying to put together in her mind the news her daughter Chen had given her today. Her husband was equally puzzled.

"Autism spectrum disorder. Never heard of it!" her husband, Han, was saying, shaking his head.

"Come on, Han. You said it yourself. Tim's odd; as if he doesn't care about people. His tantrums and fussiness drive us crazy. We're dealing with a lot more than any of our friends have to do with their grandchildren."

"What I want to know is, where were these kids when we were growing up?" Han asked. "Or did they just suddenly appear?"

Ling grew thoughtful. "Do you remember Richard Allen? He went to school with us."

"Allen? That dorky kid who wore those weird clothes? The one who raised his hand to answer every question?"

"Yeah, him. Maybe he had an autism spectrum disorder. He never seemed to have any friends. Do you remember how everyone used to make fun of him?"

Han nodded. "I wonder where Richard is now."

"You could look on the Internet." Tim's monotone suddenly broke into their conversation, without him even looking up from his train. He then proceeded to give a long lecture on how to use his favorite search engine.

It looked as if he was talking to his trains.

Welcome to the world of autism spectrum disorders! You may be grinning at Ling and Han's story because Tim sounds so much like your grandchild. There is as much to smile about as to struggle with when it comes to ASD. The great thing is that with lots of information and a bit of experience, you can help pave the way to more smiles and less struggle.

Your interest in learning about your grandchild's diagnosis is probably the greatest gift you can give him. By understanding how he sees the world, you can help guide him toward a happy and successful life.

What Is the Autism Spectrum?

Autism spectrum disorder (ASD) is a broad term to describe *pervasive development disorders* such as autism, Asperger Syndrome, childhood disintegrative disorder, Rett Syndrome, and pervasive development disorder-not otherwise specified (PDD-NOS). These neurological disorders and differences affect the child's development.

There are lots of people with ASD among us. According to the Centers for Disease Control and Prevention (www.cdc.gov), approximately one child in every 110 is on the autism spectrum. Boys are four times more likely to have an ASD than girls. Often ASD runs in families, with several family members exhibiting some traits. So your grandchild is not alone on the autism spectrum, and neither are you alone as a grandparent.

Is the Label Necessary?

Some people believe that labels (such as Asperger Syndrome, learning disabilities, etc.) make matters worse. Labels subject the child to being treated differently and stigmatize him wherever he goes. Other people believe that the label allows the child to access the right programming and helps adults provide him with what he needs.

Whether you think labeling is a good thing or a bad thing isn't important. Your grandchild already has the label. The good thing is that because of the label, schools will provide accommodations and special programming for the child. Other organizations may offer other benefits. For example, the child's parents may qualify for respite care. At the very least, the confusion is now a thing of the past. Everyone has information about the child's needs.

Asperger Syndrome and PDD-NOS

Asperger Syndrome was the original name for ASD in people who had average to above-average intelligence, named after an Austrian pediatrician, Hans Asperger. In 1944, Asperger studied and described a group of children who had good verbal skills but little ability to read body language. They also showed very little empathy and emotion, lacked friendship skills, and were physically clumsy. Asperger's work was ignored for decades until it was translated and reviewed in the 1970s by American researchers.

Since the 1970s, the definitions and descriptions of ASD have been revised many times. Indeed, some of the criteria and terminology, especially related to Asperger Syndrome, are about to change again when a new edition of the *Diagnostic and Statistical Manual of Mental Disorders (DSM-V)* is released in 2013.

Here is a table of the main traits of ASD. These won't change. Your grandchild may have all of these traits, but more likely she has just some of them.

Main Traits of ASD	
Trait	**What You Might Notice**
Above-average intelligence	• Able to learn quickly, often at an early age • Gets good grades at school • Is capable of very original (unusual) thought
Sensory issues	• Objects strongly to certain tastes, textures, sensations, smells, sounds, and types of movement • Craves certain tastes, textures, sensations, smells, sounds, and types of movement • Fidgets
Motor difficulties	• Is clumsy and has an unusual walking or running gait • Has poor handwriting and is easily frustrated by self-care tasks (e.g., tying shoe laces)
Anxiety	• Constantly frets and worries • Catastrophizes and is pessimistic
Rigidity	• Has difficulty with change and transitions • Is fearful of new things • Has fixed ideas (often wrong) that he/she refuses to change
Mind blindness	• Is unable to imagine the thoughts, feelings, and perspectives of others • Seems self-absorbed • Behaves inappropriately, failing to notice when his/her behavior angers or inconveniences others • Misunderstands what others say • Is often bewildered by human behavior
Emotional flatness and negativity	• Fails to show emotion when speaking or interacting • Is pessimistic and prone to depression • Has difficulty matching emotions to events; may have tantrums over seemingly minor events

Trait	What You Might Notice
Weak communication skills	• Has poor turn-taking and listening skills • Doesn't read nonverbal communication (body language, voice) • Interprets words and phrases very literally • Makes no or awkward eye contact
Obsessiveness	• Has one single, all-consuming interest • Has obsessions and fears • Needs to do certain things the same way every time
Social awkwardness	• Lacks true friends; doesn't know how to connect with peers • Has difficulty dealing with relationship problems • Often interacts by being silly
Lack of social awareness	• Seems unaware of surroundings or the needs of others • Fails to adapt
Weak executive function	• Has limited ability to predict, initiate, organize, plan, follow through, assess, and revise • Has difficulty controlling impulses and emotions • Has difficulty bringing details together to make a meaningful whole or to generalize facts into patterns • Focuses on details instead of the "big picture"

Who Can Diagnose ASD?

A pediatrician, psychologist, or neurologist usually makes the diagnosis. Since there's no blood test or other definitive diagnostic tool, professionals use tests and observation to determine if the child has enough traits to be considered on the autism spectrum.

While input may be sought from occupational therapists and other professionals, the official diagnosis of ASD is made by a team of school professionals.

Seeing the Child, Not the Diagnosis

First of all, your grandchild *is not* ASD. She is a *child* – with feelings, dreams, wishes, talents, and a whole lot of love to give. The diagnosis is just there to help you and her accommodate to each other. Focusing too much on the label risks turning your grandchild into a thing.

Media stories have created the perception that autism spectrum disorders are a kind of deformity or a defect. Partly that's the nature of entertainment – talk shows need to focus on the sensational and unusual to keep the ratings up. For example, it's not unusual to hear a TV personality describe a child who "suffers" from autism and then present a heart-wrenching video of a child crying miserably to himself.

Yet, autism spectrum disorders aren't a tragedy. ASD is a variation on the usual type of personality. Most children with ASD can grow up to become successful, loving adults, many with brilliant careers, provided they receive the support they need.

Above all, don't be sad. This is just life. There are no perfect children out there. Maybe it's time to think of "normal" as simply a laundry cycle.

How to Respond to Friends Who Say, "What's Wrong With Him?"

Do you tell them he has an autism spectrum disorder? It's a tricky question.

If your grandchild is an older child or a teenager, you probably shouldn't. The label is his, and he should have the right to decide who knows. But what if he's a young child?

Adults interacting with a child with ASD need to know what's going on. Otherwise, they'll likely assume, based on his behavior, that he's being arrogant, disobedient, and self-centered. Yet, when you tell people, "He's on the autism spectrum," you define him by a label.

Instead of using a label, try explaining the child. Focus on what the adult needs to know. Try, *"He has extreme difficulties with change, and his senses are turned up too high. So he feels everything too strongly. But you know, he's an absolute genius about math."* Or try, *"There's nothing wrong with him. He's got a different way of experiencing the world. Have some compassion."*

✓ Quick Tips

1. **Avoid talking about your grandchild's ASD to others in his presence:** Especially avoid talking about him in front of him, as if he's not there. He may not show that he's listening, but he can hear you. Your comments might be hurtful and confusing. If you need to talk about his issues (for example, with a teacher or professional), be sure to include him in the conversation, rather than talking as if he weren't present.

2. **Find your local services:** Many areas have autism organizations or an autism center with publicly funded programs. Some also offer fee-based services. Learn what's available.

3. **Get informed:** Magazine articles and television shows are great, but books, organizational websites, and videos often provide more information with less exaggeration and oversimplification. See the resource list on pages 127-128.

"Guess what Richard Allen's up to, Han?" Ling said with a grin after spending a half-hour on the Internet. "I found out."

"What?"

"He's a professor at a small college. He's teaching computer programming. In fact, he's the head of his department and has a lot of published papers."

"Is he married?"

"Yes. And he has two children and two grandchildren."

"How did you find all this out?"

"Well, it seems Richard's retiring this year, so he's been in the college newspaper," Ling replied. Then she grinned. "Besides, instead of tuning out that little lecture Tim gave us on using search engines, I listened, and I picked up a couple of new techniques."

Chapter 2
Too Hot, Too Cold:
Being Sensitive About Sensory Issues

Meg was babysitting her ten-year-old granddaughter Trudy so that her parents could get out for an overnight together. She'd had Trudy over from time to time before, but never for a whole night.

Mealtime was an eye opener. Meg discovered that her daughter's stories about Trudy's eating habits were true. Even at ten years old, she still ate with her fingers, obsessively wiping them after every mouthful, often on her clothes. She couldn't sit still and rarely remained in her chair for more than one bite. She yelled instead of talking. And she demanded that the dining room light be turned down because the room was too bright.

Yet what amazed Meg the most was Trudy's diet. It consisted of just twelve foods – she'd eat nothing else. No matter what Meg put on her plate, if it wasn't on the list, Trudy wouldn't eat it.

There was no other word for it – Trudy was picky, picky, picky. The temperature of the shower had to be perfect. The shampoo had to have the right smell. The towels had to be soft and free of fabric softener scent. The bed had to have cotton sheets with no wrinkles.

Meanwhile, Trudy seemed to have gone to the Boa Constrictor School of Hugs. Meg gave the child all the hugs she wanted, but sometimes her muscles were sore from all the squeezing.

By the time Trudy's parents picked her up the next morning, Meg was exhausted.

Sensory issues are often one of the first and easiest things to spot in autism spectrum disorders.

You may remember learning in grade school that the human body has five senses:

- the sense of **taste**: in the mouth
- the sense of **smell**: in the nose
- the sense of **touch**: in the skin (including in the mouth)
- the sense of **sight**: in the eyes
- the sense of **hearing**: in the ears

The human body also has two movement senses or inner senses:

- the **balance** sense (vestibular sense): in the inner ear
- the **body awareness** sense (proprioceptive sense): in the muscles and joints

Sensory difficulties occur when the senses don't communicate well with the brain. The senses send messages to the brain, but the brain can't interpret or tell the body to act on them properly. The information comes in too hard and fast, causing the brain to react in alarm, or it arrives too slow and late, causing the brain to miss key information.

The Loudspeaker and the Mute Button

You can think of your grandchild's senses as having a problem with the volume control. The volume control for some of her senses is like a *loudspeaker* – they yell at her brain in an unpleasant way. She does everything she can to get away from these sensations. These senses are often called *sensation-avoidant*[3] – because they try to avoid sensation.

2 Sensory Gang. From *Asperger Syndrome and Sensory Issues – Practical Solutions for Making Sense of the World* (Myles, Cook, Miller, Rinner, & Robbins 2000). Used with permission.

3 An internationally recognized occupational therapist, Dr. Winnie Dunn, uses many of the terms described here in her research.

"Now we have to wash your hair, Jack," Grandpa Hal said, easing the boy backward in the bathtub. "Lie back in the nice, warm water and …"

"NO!" shrieked Jack, flailing. "NO!" In his agitation, he kicked up splashes of water. One of them landed on his face. "Ah!" he screamed. "I've got water on my face! I've got water on my face! Get it off!"

The volume control for other senses is like a mute button. The senses send messages to the brain, but the brain doesn't receive them clearly. Often, the brain demands more input, craving extra sensation. These senses are often called *sensation-seeking* – because they try to seek more sensation.

Denis could never sit still. In school, he bounced around and fidgeted on his chair. At home, he pranced and hopped around the dinner table, rarely actually sitting down. His grandmother asked him why he never just sat still.

Denis looked bewildered. "My body's telling me to do this," he explained simply. "I just have to keep moving."

Children with ASD usually have a mix of sensation-avoidant and sensation-seeking senses. It's confusing to live this way, since the brain relies on the senses to help us make sense of the world. The result is a feeling of not being safe in this world.

Here is a list of the types of sensation-avoidance and sensation-seeking behaviors you might see in your grandchild.

Sensation-Avoidant and Sensation-Seeking Senses		
Sense	Sensation-Avoidant (loudspeaker is on)	Sensation-Seeking (mute button is on)
Taste	• Dislikes spices and recoils from strong flavors • Slow to try new foods • Has a very restricted diet of plain foods	• Seeks out very spicy or sour foods • Licks objects • Oblivious to burnt, rotten, or spoiled flavors
Touch	• Dislikes light touch • Dislikes the feel of certain fabrics • Avoids messy or wet activities • Avoids foods with mixed textures • Avoids busy, crowded places	• Constantly touching objects • Oblivious to food on hands or face • Seeks out messy play • Oblivious to injuries, such as cuts and bruises • Constantly poking, pushing, or touching other people
Vision	• Sensitive to sunlight and bright lights • Likes to play in the dark • Squints a lot • Dislikes making eye contact • Can't find things when they are right in front of him	• Stares a lot, especially at unusual patterns • Likes watching television and computer graphics

Sense	Sensation-Avoidant (loudspeaker is on)	Sensation-Seeking (mute button is on)
Hearing	• Easily distracted by background noise • Hums in busy or noisy environments to block out sounds • Covers ears around loud noises	• Likes loud music • Oblivious to loud noises • Says "What?" a lot
Smell	• Dislikes strong smells, even pleasant ones (smells can induce gagging)	• Craves strong smells • Often smells things
Vestibular (balance, movement through space, head position)	• Likes to have feet firmly on the ground • Dislikes elevators and escalators • Gets carsick easily • Dislikes swinging on playground equipment • Dislikes falling backward or doing somersaults	• Fidgets and has a hard time sitting still • Loves amusement park rides • Craves swinging • Jumps and bounces on any surface • Spins • Loves free-falling, being tipped upside down, and rolling
Proprioceptive (body awareness, muscles and joints)	• Overreacts to getting bumped or pushed • Dislikes pressure, such as from tight clothing • Overreacts to falling • Avoids getting hugged	• Fidgets and has a hard time sitting still • Likes to roll, bounce, crash, and squeeze • Seeks out a lot of rough-and-tumble play • Craves muscle activities, such as hanging, pushing, or pulling • May flap hands, crack knuckles, or press hands together

Felipe took the whole family out to dinner at a fancy restaurant to celebrate his retirement.

His sixteen-year-old grandson, Jorge, disliked everything on the menu and refused to eat anything except bread. The muffled sound of voices from the other tables seemed to bother him, because he kept glancing over his shoulder at the other tables and cringing. When waiters bustled by the table, accidentally brushing Jorge's chair, he became even more agitated.

"He's getting sensory overload," Felipe's daughter whispered. She looked concerned. Jorge twisted his napkin into hard knots, visibly upset.

"Jorge, why don't you go take a break outside?" Felipe said with a smile. "I don't mind. I know you find these places hard to take."

"Just wait for us on the bench by the entrance," his daughter added as Jorge got up and bolted out of the restaurant.

Twenty minutes later, when the family left the restaurant, they found Jorge sitting alone on the bench on the front porch of the restaurant, still looking upset. Once inside the car, he pulled his jacket up over his head to block out the street lights and shut out the world.

Clumsiness and Weak Muscle Control

Does your grandchild bump into furniture, tip bowls, break things, and fall down a lot? This clumsiness can be caused by vestibular and proprioceptive difficulties interfering with motor (or muscle) control. Think of the brain as the steering wheel of the body. For a child with sensory issues, this steering wheel connection is loose and wobbly, and his muscles don't respond precisely to directions.

Traits Related to Motor Control Challenges

- Difficulty avoiding walking into things because of a lack of awareness of where his body parts are relative to the furniture.

- Awkward running or walking gate, as if having difficulty keeping upright.

- Poor hand and finger movement control, such as when eating with utensils, fastening buttons and zippers, brushing teeth, combing hair, and writing.

- Difficulty doing tasks that require an arm to cross the body's midline (such as a backswing in tennis).

- Poor planning of movements, so that he uses either too much or too little force and speed.

- Poor left-right coordination.

- Difficulty forming words, leading to frustration with speaking.

The good news is that with enough exercise, stimulation, and occupational therapy, many sensitivities and motor difficulties can resolve themselves over time.[4] But in the meantime, it's a tough go for a little person.

Quick Tips

The best way to start dealing with sensory issues is to ask the child or the child's parents for information. Learn as much as you can about the child's sensory issues.

- Which senses are affected?

- Are these senses sensation-avoidant or sensation-seeking?

- What will make her more comfortable and happy?

---

4 Many occupational therapists working with children with ASD see significant improvements in their motor control after long-term therapy. See, for example, Dr. Lucy J. Miller, *Sensational Kids*, and Carol Stock Kranowitz, *The Out-of-Sync Child.*

1. **Accommodations:** If your grandchild is overly sensitive, reduce the number of irritants in the house so that she has less to deal with. Here are examples of ways you might accommodate:

   - **Clean air:** If she's sensitive to smells, avoid using strong-scented cleaning agents, wearing perfumes, or cooking strong-smelling foods. Keep the air scent-free. And if she says, "Yuck! What's that smell?" don't take it personally. Open the windows or turn on a fan. Help her find a room where the smell isn't strong.

   - **Adjustable lighting:** If she's sensitive to light, replace flickering lights with the non-flicker varieties. Hang curtains on the window so that she can adjust the amount of sunlight coming in. Allow her to wear sunglasses or a baseball cap in the house if she needs to.

   - **Calm and quiet:** If she's sensitive to sound, reduce the hum of electrical appliances and computers by turning them off or providing padding (such as a rubber mat) to absorb the vibrations. Put felt on the feet of chairs and tables so that they don't scrape against the floor. Keep a pair of earplugs or headphones handy in case she needs to retreat from the world of sound.

   - **Permission to fidget:** If she craves movement, let her fidget. This is her body's way of getting the amount of stimulation it needs. Provide a yoga ball to sit on during meals or to play on in the basement. Allow her to play with fidget toys, such as squeeze balls.

   - **Bedtime routines:** Follow your grandchild's preferred bedtime ritual and keep it the same every night. It helps her to feel calm enough to get to sleep after a bewildering day of dealing with the world. Soft, all-cotton sheets and blankets of just the right weight can sometimes also contribute to a good night's sleep.

2. **Stimulation:** Activities that stimulate your grandchild's muscles and joints by pressing or pulling may be soothing, in the way that you might find a massage or foot rub soothing. These kinds of activities stimulate the proprioceptive (body awareness) sense.[5] Keep in mind that each child is different, so what works for one might not work well for another.

- **Weighted vests and blankets:** The pressure of weights may help the child feel calm. The parents may supply a weighted vest and tell you when the child should wear it. If they don't, you can try grandpa's heavy coat, bury him under feather pillows, or let the cat sit on his lap.

- **Pressure:** Many children with sensory issues crave long, squeezy hugs. But if you're tired of giving hugs, wrap him tightly in a quilt or slowly roll a yoga ball over his back while he's lying on the floor. Always make sure he's able to breathe and talk.

- **Chores:** Pulling, lifting, pushing, stirring, and pressing all stimulate the muscles and joints in a calming and soothing way. Ensure that the tasks you come up with are well within the child's ability and are safe. Carrying a laundry basket upstairs, hanging clothes on the clothesline, walking the dog, or stirring cookie batter are all good proprioceptive tasks. You can also set up a wooden block in the basement and supervise him hammering nails into it or provide a toy hammer set.

3. **Activities:** Many kinds of physical activities are helpful.

- **Sports:** Quiet games of catch with Grandpa, or playing Frisbee, flying a kite, or trying out soccer moves will help your grandchild improve her muscle control. But avoid pushing her into organized sports.

---

5 If your grandchild is working with an occupational therapist, he may have a prescribed set of muscle exercises to do every day. Ask his parents to give you a thorough demonstration of the techniques. If the techniques are complex, you may want to consult with the occupational therapist for extra guidance.

- **Dance and fitness videos:** A young grandchild may enjoy moving to dance and fitness videos with a grandparent. The movements create lots of stimulation and help build up her nerve pathways to the brain.

4. **Great Toys for Grandma's House**

- **Marshmallow bag:** Visit an upholstery shop and ask for foam scraps. Sew two old bedsheets together to form a bag. Stuff the bag with the foam scraps and sew it closed. Your grandchild will love jumping, freefalling, crawling, and rolling in the marshmallow bag and will get a great sensory workout in the process.

- **Jumping mattress:** Instead of taking your old mattress to the dump, set it up as a jumping pad. On rainy days, help your grandchild build an obstacle course around the mattress so that she can practice motor planning, crawling, and jumping.

- **Trampoline:** If your grandchild is bouncy, she'll love a trampoline. But be sure to get the parents' permission before buying one. Also check the safety rating on the trampoline you choose. Many are poorly designed and can cause injuries.

- **Smelling center:** If your grandchild craves smell, then create a smelling center for each visit. Include cinnamon, cloves, vanilla, perfume, soap, and other pleasant scents. Leave it in the same place so she can go there to smell things when she needs to.

- **Fiddle basket:** Fill a basket with objects to fiddle with. Fiddling works the small muscles in the hands and wrists and stimulates the senses of touch and vision. Include small squeezy toys (bath toys, stress balls), clothespins, paperclips, bendable toys, pipe cleaners, fuzzy toys, and other small items that you come across during the week.

- **Play dough:** If your grandchild doesn't mind the feel of play dough or modeling clay on her hands, then sculpting is great for stimulating the hand muscles. Provide a damp wiping cloth for her hands when she wants them to feel clean again.

Quick Tips About Food

What can you do about a grandchild who won't eat your food? First, keep in mind that it's not your job to teach the child to eat a full diet. That job falls to the parents. Instead of trying to improve her eating, focus on keeping meals calm and stress-free. This low-key approach is better for you and for your grandchild.

1. **Don't take her refusals personally:** You may be a great cook, and some day in the future, your grandchild will be asking you for seconds of everything. But for now, fancy foods are impossible. She wants simple foods, well under her control.

2. **Ask the parents for a list:** The parents know exactly what your grandchild will eat. Update that list with each visit, since there may be changes. Note that brands are important. Like the princess and the pea, many children with ASD are acutely sensitive to differences in flavor and texture. If the right brand isn't at the store, the next-best brand is no substitute.

3. **Keep expectations modest:** The goal is to eat and to enjoy being together, nothing more. Your granddaughter might not be able to sit in her seat. She might not talk in a quiet voice. She might not be able to use a knife or fork properly. She might refuse to eat what you're eating. Decide that it's not a big deal. Nobody's watching, so it doesn't matter.

4. **Keep food simple:** If you don't have a list, ask your grandchild what she usually eats and choose the most nutritious items. As a general rule, sensitive eaters dislike mixed textures (e.g., sauces, casseroles, mixed pasta dishes, sandwiches) and foods

with spices or strong flavors. Stick with fresh fruit, vegetables, pastas, and simple proteins.

5. **Never insist on taking even one bite:** Taking one tiny bite is a great strategy for exploring a new food, but encourage the child – don't force her. Leave tough work to the parents. If the child is open to exploring a little, try different ways of exploring food. Maybe she can tolerate looking at it, smelling it, or touching it with a fork, or better yet, touching it to her lips. Every tiny exploration of a new food helps reduce the fear surrounding it.

6. **Think twice about restaurants:** Some children with ASD are used to eating in restaurants, but most are not. So that lunch in a restaurant that seemed like such a fun idea might not go as planned. She might find the place too noisy, the seat too uncomfortable, the food too hot, the menu too complicated, and the smells too strong. She might refuse to eat or cooperate, especially if she's tired. If you need to eat lunch while you're out, bring food with you and have a picnic somewhere quiet.

7. **Carry a comfort kit:** What you put in the comfort kit depends on your grandchild. If she has auditory sensitivities, then include earplugs; if she craves smells or gags at strong smells, then pleasant-scented objects; if she gets overwhelmed easily, then a small fiddle toy. Carry the comfort kit with you. And if travel is part of the visit, keep a kit in the car.

8. **Avoid the term "fussy eater":** It's a putdown. Remember, your grandchild is doing the best she can.

What's the GFCF Diet?

The gluten-free, casein-free (GFCF) diet means not eating wheat or milk products. It is one of the more popular non-drug treatment options for behavior issues, lack of focus, anxiety, and sensitivity.

The evidence in favor of the GFCF is largely anecdotal. There's no hard evidence. However, many families find it's beneficial. Your cooperation in following the diet will be appreciated by the parents.

Given that about 10% of the population is wheat intolerant and up to 60% is lactose intolerant (milk intolerant), there's a good chance that your grandchild can benefit from eliminating wheat or milk from his diet anyway. Eating a food that he can't digest properly is an irritant, and it adds to the stress that he's already dealing with. So even if you don't believe in it, you can be assured that it's not doing the child any harm.

What's Stimming?

Stimming is a repetitive body movement that may stimulate one or more senses. Rocking, flapping, finger tapping, and spinning are common forms of stimming. The word "stim" is short for "self-stimulation." You may do some stimming yourself sometimes. For example, drumming fingers and tapping feet when you're bored are forms of stimming.

Stimming may help your grandchild feel relaxed. Unless the stim involves hurting someone or damaging things, ignore it. Most children outgrow their need for stimulation once their body-brain connections get strong enough.

If you notice a lot of stimming, talk to the child's parents. Get their recommendations on how to handle it.

What Are Tics?

Tics are involuntary movements, like twitches. Tics are out of the child's control. The impulse comes from deep in the brain where the sensory control center is. For this reason, sensory issues and tics are related.

Common tics include throat-clearing, coughing, grimacing, shrugging, and blinking. Tics can include voice sounds, such as chirps, hoots, whistles, or repeated words. Many children outgrow their tics in adulthood.

There's not much you can do about tics. Medication treatments may help but often have side effects. Neurofeedback therapy is sometimes effective, but it's time-consuming and expensive. Some older children have gotten good results with habit reversal therapy (HRT), which involves becoming aware of tics and then slowly replacing them with more controlled movements. But in general, follow the parents' advice in dealing with tics, which may be just to ignore them.

When the Senses Are too Wound up or too Wound Down

Having senses that don't provide accurate information to the brain creates behavior problems for your grandchild. Her senses can get too wound up or too wound down and then block her thinking.

Senses too wound up: If your grandchild is in a busy environment (for example, a school fair, a competitive gym game, or a carnival), her brain's control over her senses can become disrupted. All the movement, noise, and excitement overwhelms her. She may start getting more wound up, moving more quickly and with less control. She may look agitated and bewildered, even while she's laughing and yelling. Her eyes may look wild or unfocused. Wound-up senses always end with a crash. Something gets broken, someone gets hurts, cries, or flees, or your grandchild loses it and has a meltdown.

Lou watched his grandson Aiden playing a group tag game in the gym with the other Scouts. At first, Aiden was doing well. He was getting past the bigger, faster kids, and he seemed to be having fun.

But a short while later, Lou noticed a change. Aiden was running wildly, looking desperate to dodge his attackers. He seemed agitated and less like a kid having fun. As more and more kids got tagged out, Aiden would grin briefly, enjoying his newfound status as a top player, but the grin would switch quickly to fear as he realized more kids would now be chasing him.

Lou cringed in his seat, waiting for the inevitable. He knew that the moment Aiden got tagged out, he would scream and run out of the gym.

Fortunately, Aiden's parents had talked to the Scout leader in advance. To Lou's immense relief, the leader blew the whistle, pronounced everyone a winner, and sent them all for a drink of water at the fountain. At first, Aiden still looked wound up, but after he'd had his drink, he was much more relaxed.

Senses too wound down: If your grandchild has to sit still for a long time (such as at school, in a restaurant, or watching TV), he can lose track of his body. After a while, the brain starts getting confused and anxious, and the child becomes grouchy and irritable, unable to pull himself out of the downward spiral. His body may be floppy, and he may cry. The longer he sits still, the lower and lower he gets.

Anna had been looking forward to the visit from her grandchildren all day. After all, she had added a new slide to the backyard swimming pool after her daughter told her how much eleven-year-old William loved waterslides.

As soon as they arrived, her nine-year-old granddaughter Melissa bounded out of the car and gave her grandmother a hug. •

"Where's Will?" Anna asked.

William was curled up in the back seat of the car, looking sullen and uncooperative. His mother had to pull him out of the car. He looked like a limp noodle.

"I think he'll be fine after a while," she whispered to Anna. "He's been in the car for too long. He always acts this way after long car rides."

After her daughter left, Anna tried to cajole William into putting on his bathing suit and try the new waterslide. Melissa was all ready to jump in, but Will was slouching on a deck chair, his gaze dark, his face un-moving. It was as if he couldn't even hear her. Occasionally he would make a sound, like a moan or a cry, but other than twisting a bit in the chair, he remained still and silent.

Quick Tips

Where possible, prevent your grandchild's senses from getting too wound down or too wound up by using the ideas presented above as well as the tools described in the following.

Mouth Tools

Mouth tools can be an easy and effective way to yank the sens-es back into the normal zone. They may look like snacks (see the list below) – and many are. They work by stimulating the senses in the mouth area: taste, smell, and texture. Moreover, the vestibular (balance) sense located in the inner ear is stimulated by the mov-ing jaw muscles, and the proprioceptive (body awareness) sense is stimulated by the muscle movements of the mouth.

Experiment with these mouth tools to discover which categories work best for your grandchild. Then keep some handy. But always check with the parents first to make sure the foods fit into the child's diet and they don't cause swallowing problems.

- **Chewy foods:** gum, licorice, caramels, gummy bears, jerky, dried fruit
- **Crunchy foods:** crisp fruit and vegetables, hard granola bars, cereals, cookies, nuts, popcorn
- **Fizzy drinks:** soda pop
- **Sucking foods:** drinking through a straw, frozen chocolate chips, hard candy
- **Cold foods:** ice cream, yogurt, popsicle, ice
- **Warm foods:** tea, freshly baked bread, pizza, hot chocolate
- **Sweet foods:** candy, cookies, honey
- **Sour foods:** sour candies, sweet-and-sour sauce
- **Smelling foods:** cinnamon candies, vanilla, baking bread
- **Blowing:** blowing bubbles, blowing out candles

Anna ran into the house. She grabbed a hard granola bar, poured a glass of cold orange juice, and found a straw. Then she spent a few long minutes outside persuading William to take a sip and a bite.

The coldness, chewiness, and sucking action seemed to revive him. A few minutes later, he was able to answer questions. The dark look was gone. He was sitting upright now, glancing at his sister playing in the pool.

"I have a towel," Anna said, opening it up. "Do you want me to wrap you in it?"

Will nodded. Anna wrapped him up tight, then hugged him hard. The tight hug seemed to calm him down and wake him up.

"Come on in!" Melissa shouted. "The slide's great!"

"You don't have to go in, Will," Anna said. "It's fine if you just want to watch."

But William wasted no time getting his bathing suit on and joining his sister.

Chapter 3
The Perfect Storm:
Dealing With Emotional Issues

Noor and Pramit were babysitting their nine-year-old grandchild Raj for the afternoon. On their way back from the park, they decided to stop at the grocery store to pick up a few items for supper. They didn't know that Raj's mother had never taken him to a grocery store before.

And they very quickly learned why not.

Raj seemed dazed by the colors, the stacked shelves, and all the tempting goodies. He spotted several of his favorite snacks and ran from one shelf to another. "I want that! I want that!" His eyes were bright, and his movements quick. He kept darting away from the shopping cart.

Both grandparents could see that Raj was spiralling out of control, so they decided to pay for what they already had in their cart and get out of the store as quickly as possible.

But it was already too late. When Raj learned they were leaving without buying all the treats he'd seen, his composure broke. He had a meltdown right by the checkout stand.

Customers were staring. Noor was kneeling on the floor beside him, whispering for him to get back up. Pramit was sternly reciting to him the consequences for misbehaving in public. Whenever they tried to touch him, Raj lashed back, screaming even louder. Noor started saying anything to placate him, even offering to buy him the treats that he'd wanted.

"Spoilt-rotten kid!" a woman muttered as she shoved her cart past the wailing boy and his frustrated grandparents.

Emotional Tsunamis

As pointed out in Chapter 1, children with ASD may feel things more strongly than other children. Their emotions are the same as anyone else's emotions, but their brain is not always able to process them and keep them in check   Emotions ratchet up quickly, and when they do, they overwhelm the child.

Think of the brain's emotional control center as a dike protecting a coastline and your grandchild's emotions as the powerful seas beyond. In most children, the control centers are strong, sturdy barriers that prevent all but the strongest waves from getting through. But in children with ASD, these control centers are not always effective. The tiniest underwater events can end up triggering emotional tsunamis that easily crash over the walls. The result is chaos.

Common Emotional Issues in Children With ASD	
Emotional Issue	**Description**
Anxiety	• Fear of ordinary events and objects • Constant worrying and fretting • Obsessions and fixations • Panic • Phobias and irrational fears
Resistance to Change	• Insistence on routines • Difficulty with transitions between activities • Inflexibility
Meltdowns	• Excessive anger • Lightning-fast meltdowns that seem to come out of nowhere

When dealing with emotional issues, a simple, low-key, consistent approach works best. Find out what the parents do and try to do the same thing at your house.

The Five-Point Scale

Kari Dunn-Buron and Mitzi Curtis (www.aapcpublishing.net) developed the concept of a five-point scale to help children with ASD get perspective. The child uses the five-point scale to measure how high his emotions are. Each level also tells the child how much to react, or how seriously to take the situation.

You can post a five-point scale on your fridge. When your grandchild is getting upset over a situation, point to the scale and say, "Look, your emotions are getting too high. I think they're a 3 right now. Do you think they're a 3? Let's try to get them back down to a 1."

The five-point scale is also useful for helping children decide how much they should react: Is this an ordinary event, an important situation that requires action, or an emergency?

Sample 5-Point Scale	
5	This is freaking me out. I'm losing control.
4	This is upsetting me. I want to make it stop now.
3	This makes me feel worried and anxious.
2	This bothers me a little bit, but I still feel okay.
1	This doesn't bother me. I feel calm and relaxed.

Anxiety

Anxiety involves worry and fear. It's a common issue for children with ASD.

Anxiety is like a car's engine that's idling too high. The child can't relax. Any emotional fuel that comes down the line gets burned too hot and too fast. The child is not necessarily anxious *about* anything – he is just always ready to be anxious. Unfortunately, anxiety itself becomes a feedback loop, with more anxiety and high emotions driving the idle speed higher and higher.

Where does this anxiety come from? We don't know. But we do know that it is real!

Why Does She Scream?

Many children with ASD scream more than other children, especially when they're young. They experience situations to an extreme, so everything feels like an assault and an emergency. Screaming can occur in any of the following situations:

- **Overstimulation:** Your grandchild's senses are too wound up. There's too much going on, and she can't cope. A scream may release some of the tension and confusion. Or it may signal that she needs help calming down.

- **Understimulation:** Your grandchild's senses are too wound down. He's been still and quiet for too long. The discomfort causes him to scream or start crying. (Ironically, the act of screaming may be enough to stimulate his senses to wake back up!)

- **Communication difficulties**: Many children with ASD have difficulty talking because they can't find the words. Some children also have motor difficulties in the speech muscles. Frustration builds when they want to speak and can't. Sometimes they scream as a result of that frustration.

- **Clogged emotions:** When too much emotion is coming in all at once, it can clog the child's brain, making him unable to think. Sometimes the child screams as a result of those emotions.

When your grandchild screams, she may be expressing her frustration and confusion. The scream usually doesn't last long (although it can be mortifying in public). A quick snack or some mouth tools can help get it over quickly. Removing her from the trigger situation also helps.

To prevent screaming, watch for warning signs that the tension is building. Keep your voice quiet, and say as little as possible till the tension goes down. **Agitated children often can't tolerate listening to a lot of talking.**

Quick Tips

If your grandchild has a lot of anxiety issues, his parents are likely already working on them. The child may be attending a counselling, social skills, or occupational therapy group; receiving neurofeedback therapy; or taking a prescription medication.

But unless you're a professional, at your house there won't be any fancy therapies. Instead, you can help by reducing anxiety-creating situations and making your time together as relaxed and happy as possible.

Here are some general ways to reduce your grandchild's anxiety.

1. **Keep the house calm and relaxed:** Always use a quiet, even voice with an anxious child. The calmer your voice is, the less likely it is to feed her anxiety. When you talk to the child, focus on positive topics and avoid negative topics. Children with ASD don't need to overhear you talking about the news, the neighbor's health problems, or the latest fear craze.

2. **Follow routines:** Children with ASD feel safe when they're in their routines. As much as possible, keep everything the way your grandchild is accustomed to.

3. **Use pen and paper:** Many children with ASD are visual learners, so using pen and paper helps make ideas clear to them. Part of their anxiety may come from not completely understanding what people say. Use stickman figures, circles, boxes, and checklists to present information visually.

4. **Avoid belittling comments:** As frustrating as it is to watch a ten-year-old being unable to handle a situation that a typical four-year-old can handle, keep in mind that it's even more frustrating to be that child in that situation. Lecturing, chiding, and mocking will not make the behavior go away. Instead, it will damage your grandchild's trust in you. Try to keep a cool head.

Fears and Obsessions

In addition to worrying and fretting, anxiety often creates the following types of problems:

- **Obsessive-compulsiveness:** An obsession feels like a deep, overwhelming need, and obeying that need helps your grandchild feel more calm. For example, he may have obsessive rituals regarding toys, bedtime, or hygiene. He may obsess about hand-washing because he's afraid of catching a virus. He may need to count things or line them up. You may already have noticed that your grandchild has one or two special, all-consuming interests. This interest can be a hobby or a research topic. For children with ASD, the intense special interest is a part of who they are, and it should never be discouraged.

- **Irrational fears:** Children with ASD can develop irrational fears about ordinary objects, which can cause them to scream, run, or hyperventilate. For example, a child may be so scared of dogs that she screams at the sound of a dog barking three blocks away. Or she may be so afraid of insects that she runs away from mosquitoes or flies when outside playing.

- **Panic attacks:** A panic attack is a powerful surge of fear. It often doesn't last very long – from a few seconds to a few minutes. A panic attack is physically intense and can feel like a heart attack. There's usually a trigger, but sometimes panic attacks happen for no apparent reason.

Quick Tips

1. **Help your grandchild identify his obsessions:** Don't try to stop obsessive actions. This will distress the child. Instead, help your grandchild become aware of his obsessions by gently helping him see that such actions aren't rational and serve no real-life function.

"I need to line up my books before I go to bed."

"Okay. But you know you don't really need to. They're okay where they are."

"I need to."

"Does your brain tell you that you have to?"

"Yes."

"It's a strong feeling, isn't it?"

"Yes."

"Okay. You can have two minutes to line them up. But remember, this is just a feeling. You don't really need to line the books up. They're fine where they are."

2. **Slow down the adrenaline:** When your grandchild is deal-ing with fears and panic attacks, adrenaline can make him feel short of breath and dizzy and cause him to suddenly start running or screaming. You can try the following suggestions, provided they don't make the child feel uncomfortable. As repeated throughout this book – When in doubt, check with the child's parents.

   - **Ask him to breathe slowly.** Hold him gently (unless that is uncomfortable for him) and breathe along with him. If he can do this, it will reduce the effects of the adrenaline.

   - **Give him a hug (if he is okay with it).** It's reassuring; it prevents him from running away, and it releases some of the stress. Calmly murmur kind, soothing comments as you hold the child.

   - **Offer a calming activity at the end.** Quiet music or a favorite toy or book may help him feel secure again.

Resistance to Change

Children with ASD are chronically inflexible. They insist on routine. Routines help them to feel safe in a world that's overwhelming and bewildering.

Resistance to change is a lot like a blind person always keeping everything in the house in exactly the same place. Change is like someone moving a few pieces of furniture, creating new opportunities to stumble and get confused.

How Change Feels

- **Change overloads her senses.** There are new sounds, sights, and sensations. She's learned to fear change because of the assault on her senses.

- **Change opens the door to surprises.** She dislikes not knowing what's coming up.

- **Change reduces calmness.** It pulls her out of a situation just as she was feeling relaxed and safe in it.

- **Change forces her to quit something that wasn't finished.** She needs closure; she needs to finish something before moving onto the next activity.

What's a Transition?

The word *transition* means moving from one activity to another. Putting away the video game and coming to the kitchen table for lunch is a transition. Getting off the swing and going to the slide is a transition. Your grandchild's school day is full of transitions, as the schedule moves from one subject area to another, then to recess, then to lunch, then to gym, then back to the classroom. Each transition requires her to cope with sensory overload, fears, and bewildering social situations.

✔ Quick Tips

Help your grandchild deal with transitions by preparing for them well in advance.

1. **Share the schedule:** Children with ASD feel more in control of their transitions if they know what's coming up. So share the schedule. Write it down on a piece of paper. Make sure the times are included. Your grandchild may want to draw illustrations on it, color it, or add some of her own words to it. Stick to that schedule. Don't improvise.

   An advantage to having a written, daily schedule is that you can use it to prepare the child if you have to make a change. Give her the schedule, talk about the change you need to make, and together write or draw it into the schedule.

   Your grandchild may prefer to put the schedule on a computer, iPhone, etc. You can make the file in advance and study it together when she arrives. If changes are needed, she can input them and print off the revised schedule. That way, she'll feel more in control, which will help her accept the transitions as they come up.

   In addition, the parents may have developed routines at home that you should imitate at your house. Communicate with the parents in advance if you have to change the schedule so that they can talk to the child before he arrives.

Sarah usually had her six-year-old granddaughter Tara for the afternoon on weekdays. They always followed the same schedule: watch Tara's TV show at 1:00, eat a snack at 1:30, play Tara's choice of activities at 2:00, and go to the park at 2:30.

Today, however, Sarah needed to bake some cookies for the neighborhood garage sale. So she sat down with Tara at lunch time and talked about the change. She pulled up the computer file of the regular afternoon schedule and discussed the need to fit in baking cookies. She gave Tara the computer mouse and asked her where she thought they could fit in the new activity.

After several minutes, Sarah and Tara had agreed on a plan to bake cookies instead of going to the park. Sarah printed the schedule and gave Tara some stickers to decorate it before taping it to the fridge.

Watch TV 1:00
Eat Snack 1:30
Tara's Choice 2:00
Bake Cookies 2:30

2. **Give advance notice:** Your grandchild will lose track of time, especially if he's deep into an activity. So give him adequate advance warning about the upcoming change. "Five minutes until … four minutes until …" and so forth. Just before it's time to make the transition, help him get closure on the activity he's been doing by talking about it as if it's over. Mention when he can work on it again. Then gently focus his attention on what's coming up, emphasizing the things he likes.

   "It's five minutes till dinner time. It's time to put the coloring books and crayons away. How many pictures did you finish today? Three? That's great for one afternoon!"

   Three minutes have passed.

   "Okay, now it's two minutes till dinner time. Let's put the book and crayons over here. We're having noodles for supper. Do you want me to sprinkle cheese on them or do you want them plain?"

3. **Create a "finish-later box":** A "finish-later box" is a place to put crafts and activities that got interrupted. Children with ASD dislike interruptions and feel a strong need for closure. The "finish-later box" will help your grandchild feel as if the interruption is not a catastrophe.

4. **Avoid surprises:** For many children with ASD, there's no such thing has a "pleasant" surprise. Surprises are uncontrolled events that disrupt the child's routines and the security they give her. Surprises can also be assaults on her need to know what's coming up. This means that even good surprises can be

upsetting. For the same reasons, secrets are distressing – they involve information that others have but that the child doesn't have. She doesn't like the feeling that comes from not knowing what's going on. Avoid surprises by explaining what's going to happen, even if that means explaining what's inside the present before you give it to the child.

Meltdowns

A meltdown is an emotional storm that takes over a child's entire body and mind. He loses control of his emotional state. Adults stand by helplessly while it rages on. Eventually, it ends on its own, but it can take a long time.

Some people use the word *tantrum* instead of *meltdown*. But a tantrum is generally viewed as an attention-seeking behavior that can be controlled. A meltdown is different because the child isn't in control. It may look like wilful disobedience or "spoiled-kid behavior." But look a little closer, and you'll see the panic behind the rage. A storm of emotions is assaulting the child's brain in a frightening way, and she needs help and support to get through it.

Causes of Meltdowns

Ross Greene's book *The Explosive Child* gives a superb description of meltdowns.[6] He compares the build-up phase of a meltdown to a vapor lock in a car's engine. When vapor builds up in the pipes, the fuel can't get through, and the engine stalls. In the same way, emotions building in the child with ASD flood the brain's thinking centers.

Warning Signs

Every child is different, and some meltdowns truly seem to come from out of the blue. But there are some classic warning signs.

- **The child is too wound up or too wound down:** If the child has been spinning more and more out of control, she's head-

---

6 Another useful resource is Brenda Smith Myles and Jack Southwick's book, *Asperger Syndrome and Difficult Moments: Practical Solutions for Tantrums, Rage, and Meltdowns.*

ing for a crash. Or if she's been still for too long, she feels irritable. Her body is craving sensory input and isn't getting any. The feeling of being wound up or wound down is intensely uncomfortable and can trigger a meltdown all on its own (see Chapter 2). If you add in any other factor (such as a sudden change in schedule), a meltdown is almost guaranteed.

- **The child is hyperfocused on a special interest:** When the child is absorbed in his special interest, he can be oblivious to the rest of the world. In general, this is fine. It's healthy for him to have a hobby. But when you interrupt a special activity, you can inadvertently trigger a meltdown.

- **The child's frustration is building:** If the child is trying to do an activity that's too difficult for him, or is setting standards that are too high, the result will be frustration. Young children don't know that the ideas in their heads are usually far more perfect than real life. They often insist on doing things they can't, which sets them up for a meltdown.

Perfectionism and Frustration

A tendency toward perfectionism and a low tolerance of frustration cause great stress for many children with ASD. Your grandchild might expect perfection from himself. When his handiwork is less than ideal, he might not be able to accept that. The world is not as it should be. Meanwhile, his frustration is building. His hands can't create what his mind can see. Lack of coordination, difficulty finding words, and clogged emotions add to the frustrations he has to deal with. Like two volatile chemicals in a test tube, perfectionism and frustration can result in an explosion.

- **The child looks agitated:** Unfocused eyes, jerky movements, and a rising voice are all signs of emotions building. Your grandchild may also be prancing or flapping his hands. He may do the same actions over and over (for example, pounding on the computer keyboard) or repeat the same words (*"It isn't working! It isn't working! It isn't working!"*). This is the "vapor lock" we talked about earlier – his thoughts can't flow; he's stuck.

- **The child has difficulty finding words:** Children with ASD often have difficulty retrieving words when they want to speak. When the child is emotionally distraught, finding the right words to say becomes even harder – exactly when he desperately needs to communicate his distress. Instead of telling you what's wrong, he may simply repeat the same word over and over, yell irrational comments that have nothing to do with the problem, scream, or make helpless, fearful sounds.

Quick Tips for Preventing a Meltdown

An ounce of prevention is worth a pound of cure. Learn to divert a meltdown before it happens.

1. **Share the schedule:** Change, interruptions, and transitions can trigger a meltdown. Reduce the chances of a change-related meltdown by involving your grandchild in planning the day and sticking to the schedule. Even if things are going well, avoid the temptation to extend an activity.

2. **Avoid overstimulation:** Respect your grandchild's limits. Avoid overstimulating him with too much activity. It may seem like a great idea to go to the park in the morning and the zoo in the afternoon, but that's two big events in one day. On top of the fatigue, he might get anxious dealing with all the new sensations. Don't try to do too much. Save some good ideas for another day.

3. **Provide a quiet place:** Make sure there's a quiet and safe place your grandchild can run to when he feels frustration building. Let him close the door and stay quiet till he calms himself down. This may strike you as running away from the problem, but it isn't. He has recognized a problem, realized that he can't handle it, and taken steps to get himself under control.

4. **Keep mouth tools and fidget toys handy:** Mouth tools and fidget toys (see Chapter 2) work well for calming agitated senses and emotions. Ensure that you always have some mouth tools with you; you never know what might happen.

5. **Talk him down from the edge:** Get involved early to head off a meltdown. Your grandchild can't access his ability to think right now, so you have to provide his missing thoughts. For some children, it is helpful to talk in a calm, quiet voice as if you're the voice of his brain. Help him gain balance and perspective.

"I hate this computer!"

"Hate is a strong feeling. You're having strong feelings right now. Do you really mean you hate it, or that you're angry with it?"

"I hate everything!"

"Your anger is spreading to things that aren't causing problems. Let's keep the anger just for the computer. What's it doing?"

"It's crashing all the time!"

"You've fixed crashes before. You're very good at fixing computers. You're good at figuring out what's wrong. Maybe, just maybe, you can fix it."

"No, I can't! Not unless I reboot it!"

"It's maddening, isn't it? You probably feel angry about that. Rebooting takes time. Maybe you're angry mostly because you have to reboot when you don't want to. I wonder when they'll invent a computer that doesn't crash."

"Probably never! This is going to take another five minutes to reboot!"

"So that means we have five minutes. How about we reboot it and go get a granola bar while we wait?"

6. **Turn it into a game:** Some children with ASD balk at any command. Instead of letting the showdown turn into a meltdown, you can turn it into a game.

    "Jennie, for the third time, I'm telling you that you have to clean up this mess."

    "No! I won't do it!"

    Mina stood in the doorway and thought for a moment. She knew that if she kept pressing six-year-old Jennie, she'd blow up. It was time to change tactics.

    "I wonder what would happen if I just stop telling you this and go downstairs for a few minutes, then come back upstairs," she said quietly. "I wonder what might happen."

    Jennie glanced up but didn't make any move to start cleaning.

    Mina went downstairs and made a small snack of two mouth tools – a chewy bar and a glass of milk with a straw. Standing at the bottom of the stairs, she said loudly, "Here I am with this great snack, and I'm about to walk upstairs. I wonder what I'll see."

    She could hear Jennie scrambling and gave her another minute. Then she walked loudly and slowly up the stairs.

    She smiled. Jennie had made an effort to clean the mess. It wasn't perfect, but it would do for today. Mina gave her a hug and presented her granddaughter with the snack.

7. **Distract him:** Find an article or small toy related to your grandchild's special interest. Keep it handy. When a meltdown threatens, try to distract him by presenting your find.

8. **Ask the parents for advice in advance:** The parents can tell you the signs of an approaching meltdown. They can also tell you what prevention techniques work best for them.

Quick Tips for Dealing With a Meltdown

A meltdown in public is mortifying. You feel as if everyone is staring at you, and you feel helpless. The best tip for dealing with meltdowns is to focus on the child, not on yourself. Forget about your feelings. Forget about what other people are thinking about you. Stay calm and provide your grandchild with what he needs.

1. **Keep your voice calm:** Don't yell, raise your voice, wheedle, or beg when your grandchild is in the throes of a meltdown. Staying calm is the hardest thing in the world to do, but it's very important. Becoming emotional is like throwing water on an oil fire – it just spreads the flames. Your grandchild is already overwhelmed by his own emotions, so he can't possibly process yours as well.

2. **Think out loud for him:** Picture yourself as the thinking part of the child's brain. Provide the thoughts he needs to wrestle his emotions back in check.
   - **Acknowledge how he feels.** *"You're feeling overwhelmed right now. Your feelings are too much, and you don't know what to do with them. You don't like screaming like that."*
   - **Encourage him.** *"You can do it! You've done it before."*
   - **Describe the steps he needs to take.** *"First, you need to take some deep breaths. That will help make the screaming go away. Can you breathe with me? Let's take some breaths. That's great! Now, why don't you try squeezing my hand? See if you can squeeze all those feelings into me ..."*

3. **Protect him from injury:** Young children may need protection from injury, especially if they spin or run around during a meltdown. Avoid grabbing your grandchild unless you absolutely have to. If you can get her into a soothing hug, she will calm down faster.

4. **Provide a soothing or distracting activity afterward:** Once the child seems to be regaining composure, quietly offer a

drink or snack, or a favorite toy. Say as little as possible so that he can let his brain rest. If possible, move the child to a quiet, safe place where you both can recover. Avoid raising your voice, lecturing, or rushing the exhausted child, as this may trigger another meltdown.

Noor stared at her grandson Raj lying wailing on the supermarket floor. She knelt down close to him and gently put a hand on his shoulder, her face close to his. When he let her, she cupped his face.

In a soothing voice, she repeated softly, "Look at me, Raj. Look at me. Everything's okay."

He sobbed, but his flailing slowed.

"You're doing fine. Grandpa and I are both here. Let's just take some deep breaths. I'll help you."

Noor stopped being aware of the other customers. She turned her head and quietly told Pramit to look in her purse for some chewy licorice – Raj's most effective mouth tool.

A few minutes later, Raj was sitting up, hiccuping, and chewing on his licorice. Pramit also found the comfort kit and handed Raj a squishy ball to hold.

Noor took some deep breaths and stood up. "Next time we go to the supermarket," she said to Pramit, "we don't take Raj inside the store. You and he can run around on the sidewalk."

"Thank goodness we had the mouth tools and the comfort kit."

Chapter 4
Social Situations:
Becoming a Seeing-Eye Dog

Jennie watched her grandson Kyle with concern. At ten years old, he was enrolled in the gifted program at school. Not surprising, since he'd started reading books when he was just three years old! His grasp of science and technology was extraordinary. He would sit and chat with experts as if they were equals.

And yet . . .

Jennie sighed.

He had no friends. According to his mother, whenever Kyle was with peers, he would ignore them. Sometimes he'd try to talk to them, but he'd do it poorly. Most of the time he was silly or inappropriate. He had no idea how to talk about anything except science. And even then, it wasn't a conversation – just a monologue. Not surprisingly, the other kids didn't like playing with him.

Jennie was afraid to bring him anywhere in public because she couldn't predict how he would act. She felt guilty about that, but there had been too many shocks and surprises in the past. Better safe than sorry.

Yet somehow she knew they were both missing out on something important.

Imagine what it's like to be blind. Close your eyes and try to walk around the room or manage some simple tasks.

It's hard.

Now imagine being blind, not to seeing *things* but to *the idea that other people have thoughts* – to the awareness that they have opinions, ideas, needs, and wants. And even if you're made aware, you have no idea what those opinions, ideas, needs, and wants are.

Theory of mind – the ability to think about other people's perspectives – is the basis of all social interaction. You have to have a sense of another person to act socially with him. So the *mind blindness* of ASD is a major social handicap.

Why do children with ASD have problems taking others' perspectives? It may be due to brain wiring, but sensory and emotional issues may also be part of it. Babies with ASD tend to withdraw from the world instead of observing, listening, and experiencing. They fail to develop theory of mind even though their baby brains are primed to learn it.

Your grandchild can learn social skills and theory of mind, but it's much harder now that he is older. It's like trying to build the foundation of a house after the walls and roof are already up.

Theory of Mind	
Theory of Mind Skill	**Theory of Mind Challenge**
Reading facial expressions, voice intonation, and body language	• Misreading social situations because of failure to "read" people
Anticipating someone's thoughts	• Being surprised at people's expectations
Sensitivity about other people's opinions, needs, and ideas	• Valuing facts over relationships
Making friends	• Poor friendship skills • Preferring to be alone
Repairing problems in friendships	• Inadvertently sabotaging friendships and ignoring easily solvable problems

Theory of Mind Skill	Lack of Theory of Mind
Sharing, taking turns, and reciprocating	• Self-absorption
Asking for and offering help	• Lack of awareness of connection to others
Accepting criticism and suggestions	• Bristling at criticism as if attacked
Avoiding and resolving conflict	• Ignoring or blindly walking into conflict
Tact	• Rudeness • Lack of awareness of unwritten social rules

A Cat Living in a Dog World

In her book *All Cats Have Asperger Syndrome*, Kathy Hoopman illustrates how the autism personality is similar to the cat personality. Cats are aloof, detached from others, and independent. While they like to be cuddled, they lack any need to be part of a group. In contrast, most typical children are like dogs, seeking the group, wanting to fit in, looking to the leaders to obey.

You can think of your grandchild with ASD as a cat living among dogs. He has to cope with having an entirely different set of instincts from other children.

- **"Pack" instinct:** Social beings grow up learning how to please the pack and fit in. But children with ASD often don't care or are unaware of what the group likes. They like their own interests. They may want to fit in, but they don't know how.

- **Obedience instinct:** Most children instinctively understand that adults take care of children and tell them what to do. As they get older, they pick up on the body language of authority. But children with ASD don't have the instinct to follow a leader and can't read authoritative body language. As a result, many don't understand why adults get to "boss" children around, as they view it.

- **Social awareness:** Most children remain aware of the people around them at all times, including the adults. But children with ASD don't instinctively notice who's nearby, any more than they notice the furniture.

- **Give-and-take cooperation:** Most children value their place in the social group. They learn to share and to give and take. But children with ASD don't feel their place in the social group. So it's hard work for them to see the value of sharing or give-and-take.

Becoming a Seeing-Eye Dog

Grandparents can learn to act as the dog that guides the cat. They can help their grandchild navigate around their mind blindness by narrating social situations in a stage whisper, pointing out social obstacles before they arrive, and describing what they see in people's faces. They can also explain what other people expect, what they assume, and what they know (or don't know).

By guiding your grandchild gently through social situations, you can become his theory of mind. Over time, he may start to think that way on his own.

What to Say to Friends Who Say, "He's so rude!"

Children with ASD aren't rude on purpose. They lack the social aware-ness and knowledge to understand when their words or actions are rude or tactless. Often, they're just answering your question.

"Tony, you don't find this concert very exciting, do you?"

"Nope, it's totally boring. This place sucks. I want to go home."

Well ... you asked.

Try describing mind blindness to help your friends understand:

"Tony doesn't know what you're thinking or feeling, so he can't fig-ure out what's rude. He's delayed in figuring out the social rules. But he's working on it. He knows that he has to use manners words, like "please." But managing his tone of voice and face and finding the words that won't offend other people is still beyond him." You can add that honesty and literalness are the traits of a good person, ones that you don't want your grandchild to abandon.

Quick Tips

Being a seeing-eye dog to your grandchild can help you both when you're out in public and at home. Here are some ideas to try.

1. **Listen:** Your grandchild does try to explain. Beware of dismiss-ing her explanations as "talking back" or "making excuses."

   Jane took Kevin's hand and pulled him around to face her. "Listen, Kevin," she said calmly, looking straight into his seven-year-old eyes. "We're going into the doctor's office. I need you to be quiet. You can read your book and chew your gum, but don't talk to the other people in the room. In waiting rooms, people wait quietly."

   Kevin nodded. Jane opened the door to the reception area and walked up to the counter. In a flash, Kevin had walked over to an elderly man sitting in the waiting area and started reciting to him

the names of all the characters in his favorite video games. Exasperated, Jane left the counter, grabbed Kevin by the hand, and
drew him back out into the hallway.

"What did I just say? Didn't we decide that you wouldn't talk to the
people in the waiting room?"

"I don't know why I did it. It just happened."

Jane was about to give Kevin a full dressing down for being
disobedient, but then something occurred to her. Maybe he was
describing impulsivity.

"Kevin, when your body tells you to do things, what does it feel
like?"

"It feels like I can't think. I can't stop myself from doing things."

Jane wondered if that was what impulsivity felt like. She'd have
to talk to Kevin's mother about it. What a good thing she listened
before she scolded Kevin, likely for something he had little control
over!

2. **Explain roles:** Before going on an outing or entering a new
    situation, talk about the roles of people your grandchild is
    likely to encounter. What people will be there and what jobs
    will they have? What responsibilities do those jobs involve?
    Add more information as situations come up.

    Maria remembered the last time she brought Ben to the grocery
    store to pick up a few last-minute items. As they'd stood in the "8
    items or less" line, Ben had somehow noticed that the man in front
    of them was placing twelve items on the counter. Without saying
    a word, he'd started grabbing the man's purchases and tossing
    them back into the cart. Not surprisingly, the man had become
    angry. So had Ben. Maria had ended up carrying the wailing,
    indignant boy out to the car without buying anything.

    That was not going to happen today.

    She stopped the cart a good distance from the check-out lines.

"Do you see the sign for 8 items or less?" she asked Ben, pointing toward the express line.

"Yes."

"That sign belongs to the cashier. She's the boss of that line. She gets to decide what people do. Do you remember the man who was going through that line with twelve items?"

"Yes. He wasn't obeying the sign. He was breaking the rules. I was trying to stop him, but then you carried me out."

"Because it's the cashier's sign. She's the only person who gets to tell people they can't go in her line. She's the boss of her line."

"But he had twelve items!"

"If she decides it's okay, then it's okay. She's the only person who gets to tell people what to do in her line. Maybe the man was sick. Maybe the store was very busy and she didn't want him to have to go through a long line for just twelve items. It doesn't matter. She gets to decide."

"Is that why you were angry with me?"

"I wasn't angry. I just had to get you out of there. You were trying to be the boss of the line. But it's not your sign or your line. So you can't be the boss. Does that make sense?"

"Sort of."

"So are you ready to go through the line now?"

"Okay."

Being a Good Sport

Taking turns, following rules, and being gracious about winning or losing are hard skills for any child to learn. For your grandchild with ASD, they're especially hard. Children with ASD don't instinctively value their relationship with the people they're playing with, so they don't give in when something strikes them as unfair. And they can't see their behavior from the perspective of the other players.

You can help your grandchild learn game skills by playing games with him. The basic rule of games is "friends before points." In other words, game-playing is a *double game*; it includes the board/sports game and an invisible friendship game. In the friendship game, you get points for being cheerful, cooperative, and gracious, and you lose points for being argumentative, dishonest, and complaining. It's more important to win the friendship game than to win the board/sports game.

3. **Insist on good manners:** *Please, thank you, you're welcome, excuse me*, and *pardon me* are phrases that every child can get in the habit of using. Prompt your grandchild to include these words if he forgets. You can also prompt him about polite behavior, with phrases such as *Ask before taking something*, and *Wait your turn*. Over time, your grandchild will start to remember without the prompting.

4. **Explain, using stick-figure cartoons:** Sometimes words alone can't explain complex social situations, especially when the child needs to understand the perspectives of several people. Draw stick figures to represent each person, then draw thought bubbles to show their thoughts. Show what they're looking at (with dotted lines from the eyes) and add simple facial expressions (smile, frown, tear). Add speech bubbles if necessary.

5. **Brainstorm multiple causes for behaviors:** Many children with ASD make false conclusions and then can't adjust them as new information becomes available. You can help your grandchild break out of rigid thinking patterns by showing him how to consider many possible causes for someone's behavior.

   "Dimitri doesn't want me to come over! He hates me!"

   "That's one possible reason. But there are other possibilities, too. Maybe he's sick. Maybe he already has a friend over. Or maybe his mom wants him to do his homework. What other reasons could there be?"

6. **Explain friendship:** Children with ASD, especially when very young, tend to see a friend as a thing or possession. Your grandchild may assume that friendship just means two people who are in the same place at the same time, or two people who have talked with each other. She may not realize that friendship is about *connection, shared history,* and *shared fun.*

   Children need to learn that they can make and keep friends because of what they *do and say* and how well they treat others. To have a friend, they have to *be* a friend. You can help your grandchild by talking about friendship and advising him in his efforts to find friends.

Deepening Your Relationship With Your Grandchild

You may have dreamed of having a very special relationship with your grandchild. He was so sweet and tiny when he was born! Years have passed, and you and your grandchild seem to suffer from a bewildering lack of connection. You desire a deeper connection, and so does he on some level, but you don't know how to get past the social challenges. There are things you can do to foster that connection. They all involve letting the child take the lead and you following.

Connecting With a Young Child

The younger your grandchild is when you start making a connection with her, the more you help her social development. The more adults who engage her, the more she'll grow up understanding relationships.

Stanley Greenspan and Serena Wieder's book *Engaging Autism* offers many suggestions for connecting with young children on the spectrum. Their basic advice is to start where the child is, making simple efforts to connect and finding ways to share fun.

1. **Floortime play:** The "floortime" method is a popular way of engaging young children in shared play. You need to get down on the floor with the child, at eye level with her. If floor level is awkward for you, sit down across from the child when she's playing at a table. She may not notice you because she's absorbed in her play. Make quiet, gentle attempts to engage her attention. For example, ask questions about what she's doing or comment on what you see her doing. Offer no criticism, teaching, correction, or advice. The goal is simply to be where her mind is.

Ella watched three-year-old Tammy playing with her trains. She lay down on the floor beside her, propping up her head with her hand. "You're playing with your blue train and green train," she said quietly. "Are they your best trains?"

"Yes," Tammy answered without looking up. She said nothing more, so Ella simply continued watching for a few minutes. Tammy proceeded to smash the two trains together.

"Does the blue train feel sad when the green train does that?"

"No, he likes it."

"Does the green train like it, too?"

"Yes."

Little conversations like this may be enough for one day. Get the child used to having you there beside her, talking about her play. Over time, she may start telling you what she's doing, rather than waiting for you to ask.

Eventually, you can try to engage the child in simple shared play. Pick up a toy and gently approach her playing, talking quietly or making play noises. At first, she might pull back or turn away. If she does, then rest for a minute before trying again. Your goal is to make a connection between her play and your play.

"Can my red train follow your green train? She'd like to follow him to the train station."

"Okay."

Ella pushed her red train along the track, but as she did, Tammy swerved her train right off the track instead of going to the station.

"Should the red train turn here, too?"

Tammy said nothing, but she'd turned her back to Ella. After a few minutes, Ella left the red train on the track and picked up one of the peg people from the builder set.

"This girl likes to watch the trains go by. Can she sit beside the track and watch?"

"Yes."

"Is there a special place where she should sit?"

"She can sit there." Tammy pointed to a spot on the carpet. Ella moved the toy accordingly. After a few minutes, she asked, "Can the girl push the yellow train to go beside the green train?"

Later, you can create little play problems and solve them together: *"The red train is hungry. What should we do?"* By concentrating on connecting with your grandchild in her own world, you'll have a much better chance of engaging her and drawing her out.

2. **Hold hands while playing:** Young children with ASD often like to jump, crash, swing, and climb (see Chapter 2). You can turn these activities into shared moments by holding hands and making eye contact while doing them. Try counting *1–2–3* before starting to help the child coordinate her fun with yours. When playing on a swing, give her some high-fives. Your goal is to get her to share her enjoyment with you.

3. **Play simple social skills games:** Many programs teach kids how to "do" social skills by memorizing a rule or practicing a pattern. These programs are helpful, but people can't be expected to follow scripts their entire life. You can help your grandchild by playing simple social skills games that focus on connecting, rather than on performing.

   - **Face games.** With a toddler, look him in the face, smile, and talk silly to him. If he breaks your gaze, wait a minute, then try again. Your goal is to get him to make eye contact with you and smile or laugh.

- **Finger games and lap games.** Bounce the child on your knee while singing "Pony Boy" or play "This Little Piggy" with his toes or "Itzy Bitzy Spider" with his fingers. Make as much eye contact as possible. Your goal is to create some shared fun.

- **Pretend games.** Draw out your grandchild's imagination through simple role-playing games with toys. You can use dolls, wooden peg people, Lego figurines, or play dough creations. Follow your grandchild's lead, and talk about how each of the toys thinks and feels.

Connecting With a Teen

Older children and teens need help figuring out their social world. This is an opportunity for a grandparent to make a connection. You can be the explainer, the go-to person when your grandchild needs answers.

1. **Set aside one-on-one time:** Teens with ASD are usually very good in one-on-one interactions with adults. Make time for simple outings to low-stress places where the two of you can just be together. For example, you can go watch a hockey game, walk to the store, buy some ice cream from the ice cream truck and eat it in the park, or watch birds. The activities don't have to be long. In fact, a short, pleasant activity is much better than a long activity that ends in frustration.

2. **Be a confidante:** A teen with ASD can always use someone to talk to. You can set aside time for a regular phone call to talk. Be warm and supportive. Offer to role-play upcoming situations so that he can practice.

3. **Participate in his pet interest:** Your grandchild's current special interest is the best way to connect with him. Find books and online articles about it that you can talk about. Go to community activities focused around the special interest.

4. **Practice shared problem-solving:** Shared problem-solving is an essential friendship skill. Create opportunities to work together on longer-term projects that involve solving problems (for example, building a deck chair or planting a garden). Work on solving the problems together.

5. **Follow her suggestions:** Let your grandchild make suggestions for activities to do together. Follow her suggestion instead of making her follow yours. As problems arise, solve them together so that her idea can be successful.

6. **Learn to use the Internet and how to play video games:** Many teens with ASD tend to live on the computer. You're more likely to connect with your teenage grandchild through Internet social media than through regular conversation, so don't pass up this opportunity. Ask him to teach you to play his favorite video games so that you always have an activity you can do together.

7. **Practice give-and-take:** Relationships should never be one-sided. Avoid the temptation to make the relationship all about your grandchild. After you listen to her, make sure that she understands that she has to listen to you, too. You can make your "problems" very simple (*"I can't reach up to get the bowls from the high cupboard."*) to create an opportunity for your grandchild to offer to help you. This kind of interaction reinforces the give-and-take of good relationships.

8. **Share your memories:** Teens with ASD appreciate hearing that other people had a hard time in high school. Share your stories about the time you goofed up, blurted out the wrong thing, or tripped over your feet. Be sure to finish the story by explaining how you resolved the issue, what happened the next day, and what you learned. In addition to helping your grandchild get a perspective on high school drama, you help build a connection based on common experiences.

Juanita decided to make some changes to her relationship with her grandchild Kyle. First, she created accounts on three of his favorite online social media sites. Then she asked him to help her figure them out. He was eager to show her. Afterward, she asked if he could be her online friend to help her get used to it all.

In a very short time, they became online buddies. Kyle would message her about his ups and downs at school. Juanita would offer sympathy and advice, while still making some time to talk about her own life.

"I know I have high grades and all that," Kyle typed one day, "but I don't have any friends. I'd really like to have friends. But it's impossible."

Juanita messaged back: "Why do you think it's impossible?"

"Because you have to be cool to have friends," he wrote back. "Kids who aren't cool are outsiders. They don't get friends."

"But what about all the other outsiders? Why can't they be friends with each other?"

"They can't. Only cool kids can have friends."

Juanita reread his message in amazement. No wonder Kyle didn't have any friends! He didn't think he was allowed to have any.

Over the next few days, she messaged with Kyle to broaden his understanding of friendship. Then she was able to guide him in approaching one of the other "outsiders" to invite him over to play video games. Because the lines of communication were open between them, she was able to open his world to friendship.

Chapter 5
Self-Regulation:
Focusing the Executive Function

Maria folded her arms. "I said it's time to put your computer games away. Your mother will be here in 15 minutes."

Her twelve-year-old grandson Dean glanced her way. "Okay!"

Satisfied, Maria went back to her crossword puzzle. But when she looked up two minutes later, Dean was still sitting in the same spot. "Dean!" she cried out, exasperated. "I said to clean up your games! But you haven't done anything!"

"Oh, yeah. I forgot."

"Please do it right now!"

Dean glanced unhappily at his controllers and cords. "There's too much. I don't know what to do."

"Come on, Dean! Figure it out! Just pick up all that stuff and put it in your backpack!"

Reluctantly, Dean started to move. He unzipped his backpack and pushed in a couple of cords. Maria went back to her puzzle but checked in again a minute later.

Dean was now reading a comic book he'd found in his backpack. The controllers and remaining cords still lay scattered on the floor. Maria was ready to scream in frustration.

"Dean!"

He looked up in surprise. "What?"

As exasperating as it is, the lack of focus and organization of children with ASD isn't deliberate. They are not trying to get out of chores. They lack the kind of control they need over their brain to do it.

The command-and-control center of the brain is found in the frontal lobe, right behind the forehead. The frontal lobe takes care of managing the brain so that it can do complex tasks. The ability to command your brain to do what you want it to do is called *executive function*. In children with ASD and in many adults, executive function is weak.

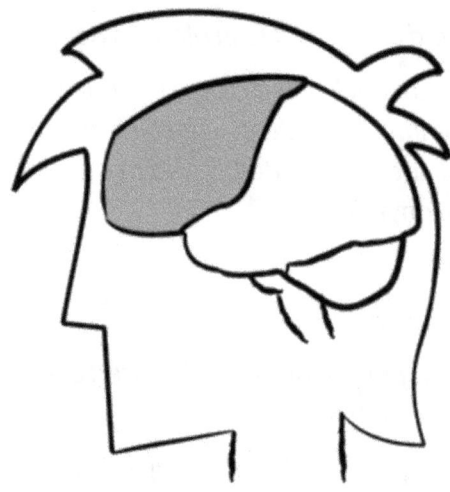

Weakness in executive function is a significant impairment in ASD. While each part of the brain can think just fine, there's nothing pulling it all together. This lack of cohesion creates problems with focus and perspective.

Weaknesses in Executive Function	
Executive Function Skills	**Weakness in Executive Function Skills**
Ability to plan, initiate, and execute tasks in a controlled manner	• Is disorganized, forgetful, and messy • Makes plans but doesn't follow them • Starts activities but rarely completes them • Has difficulty making decisions • Is unable to break a task down into steps
Ability to regulate emotions and motivation	• Gets wound up or wound down and can't get back to normal • Loses control of emotions very quickly and can't get them back under control • Can't force himself to do what he has to do • Has difficulty resisting temptation or delaying gratification • Can seem impulsive • Has difficulty staying alert or sustaining effort
Ability to focus and remember	• Has difficulty focusing, listening, or remembering what was said • Has difficulty learning from experience to avoid making the same mistakes twice • Has difficulty thinking about several things at once or using past knowledge to assess a present situation • Has difficulty evaluating actions and making changes
Ability to see general patterns, understand how the self relates to others, and do the right thing	• Appears self-centered and self-absorbed • Seems to lack empathy and ethics • Has ineffective social skills and social interaction skills • Has difficulty seeing the big picture
Mental flexibility	• Has difficulty assessing and adjusting actions to fit the circumstances • Has difficulty adapting behavior to circumstances • Has difficulty changing his conclusions

Having weak executive function is like being a ship with a sleeping captain and a loose steering wheel. No matter how hard the crew works, the ship won't get where it's supposed to go.

"Jessie, put your lunch bag up on the counter, sweetie!" Lisette called to her seven-year-old granddaughter who was untying her shoes by the door after school.

"Okay, Nana!" Lisette heard Jessie unzip her backpack. Then she heard a wail.

"What's wrong?"

"I don't have my lunch bag!" Jessie cried and sat down on the floor in utter confusion.

Lisette came over, took the backpack, and looked inside. "No, I guess you forgot it at school."

"I think I lost it on the bus!" Jessie said unhappily.

"Did you take it out of your backpack on the bus?"

Jessie nodded.

"You're not supposed to. You're supposed to zip your bag and keep it closed till you get home. Remember? That's the rule."

"I forgot!"

Jessie took the backpack and fished around in it. She pulled out a running shoe. "This is Kevin's."

"Why do you have Kevin's shoe?"

"I don't know. I don't know how it got in there."

"Well, I'll call the bus company and see if they found your lunch bag. But you did bring home your homework, right?"

Jessie fished around in the backpack again. Then there was another wail. "I left it on my desk!"

How to Respond to Friends Who Ask, "Does She Have ADHD?"

Both children with ADHD and those with ASD have challenges in executive function. Your friend is just trying to figure out what's going on. You can simply reply: *"She has difficulties with her executive function, which is the steering wheel of the brain. Kids with ADHD have the same challenges."*

Aspects of Weak Executive Functioning

- **Planning, initiating, and finishing:** You might have discovered that your grandchild gets great ideas, but they're all wings and no landing gear. Her executive function isn't strong enough to pull everything together. To add to the confusion, without executive function, she has a hard time making decisions and prioritizing (what comes first, what's most important, etc.).

- **Regulating emotions and getting motivated:** Chapter 2 explained how your grandchild can get too wound up or too wound down. Her brain has difficulty monitoring how she's feeling and making adjustments accordingly. In addition, she may suffer from boredom. Children with ASD get bored easily, because they can't step back and figure out what they could be doing. When they do start getting bored, they just spiral into deeper and deeper boredom.

- **Focusing and remembering:** Of course, your grandchild can focus and remember – she just can't always do it when she needs to. Her brain sometimes has a hard time holding several thoughts together at the same time. In social situations, it's difficult for her to keep track of everything she knows about everyone in the room. If she thinks about one thing, another one doesn't get her attention.

- **Generalizing and forming patterns:** Many children with ASD see specific items but not general patterns. For example, they'll learn the social rules for talking to Mrs. Smith and Mr. Romero at school but then fail to understand that this is the way to talk to all teachers. For this reason, your grandchild may not be learning from her experiences in the way you assume she is.

Eight-year-old Emmett let go of Sophia's hand and started running around the hardware store. It took her a few minutes to catch up to him.

She grabbed him. "Emmett! Stop running around the store touching things! Remember last week when we went to the grocery store? I told you the rule is that you stay with Grandma and don't touch."

Emmett gave her a bewildered look. "But that was for a grocery store."

"The rules are the same for any store."

"Any store? You didn't say that! How was I supposed to know?"

Quick Tips

A general strategy for organization and focus difficulties is to move the executive function outside your grandchild's brain, so to speak. For example, post it on the wall, write it down on paper, develop it into routines, or become his executive function yourself. Over time, he'll learn to do at least some of it in his head.

1. **Use lists and schedules:** Chapter 4 described how to use lists and schedules to help your grandchild focus. Make sure your lists are checklists, with a place for her to check off tasks she's finished. Checking the items helps her feel good about her progress and makes it easier to see what is left to do.

2. **Use timers:** Timers help children focus and get organized. Instead of simply giving a task and waiting for your grandchild to organize himself to do it, give him two minutes on the timer. Offer a reward for finishing before the bell if you like.

    Be aware that some children like to set the timers themselves because they don't like feeling controlled by other people. Other children may need to use the timer backwards (timing up from zero). These children get so focused on the passage of seconds that they can't focus on the task. Timing up from zero is like racking up points in a video game, something most children with ASD know very well. You can keep a record of the best times.

3. **Write down rules and post them on the fridge:** The old adage "Out of sight, out of mind" is especially true for your grandchild. If you want rules to be followed, make sure they're in plain sight. It's best if the child writes them himself, since he then can't really complain that he didn't know – even if he might try. He can also be the person to add any new rules as they come up.

4. **Develop routines for new tasks:** You might assume that your grandchild knows how to do a task because he did a similar one in the past. But you might be wrong. If the task is in any way different, don't assume he's aware of similarities. Sit down with him and describe the new task. Tell him what tasks it's similar to. Together, develop a routine for this new task. Write it down to break the work into steps.

The Ten-Second Room Zoom[7]

Most children with ASD are oblivious to their surroundings. Who's nearby? What are they doing? What objects are nearby? Are any of them dangerous? In fact, they often walk into new situations without so much as a glance around to see where they are.

When you're taking your grandchild on an outing to a new place, practice doing the Ten-Second Room Zoom. Stop at the entrance-way and together scan the situation. Narrate what you're thinking as you're looking around:

"This room looks really full of people. That means we have to move slowly and carefully or we'll bump into people. Do you see how some people are sitting, and some are standing? We should figure out whether we should sit or stand. What do you see?"

Scanning a situation before entering it is a good habit to teach to children. It will raise their awareness of their surroundings, reduce social problems, and help them match their actions to a given situation.

---

7 The Ten-Second Room Zoom is an awareness technique in *Comic Sense* by Nancy Mucklow.

5. **Prepare together:** Help your grandchild develop better executive function by involving her in planning an outing. Avoid making the plans yourself and hoping she'll just tag along. Before leaving the house, talk about where you're going. Give her as clear a picture of the situation as you can, while pointing out that things change and you can't guarantee your information is perfect. After you return home, together assess how well the outing went. List the successes as well as the difficulties. Decide what you both need to do differently to make the next outing even more successful.

6. **Use pen and paper:** Many children with ASD need to see patterns. Use pen and paper to sort similar tasks and situations into categories. Together, list the rules that apply to everything in a category. List pros and cons to help develop prioritizing skills.

7. **Avoid offering too many choices:** When there are too many options, your grandchild has too much information to sort out. Sure, it's good to give him practice choosing between inconsequential differences *("Do you want to use the red one or the blue one?")*, but be aware that even small choices can end up taking a lot of time. When your grandchild has to make decisions, keep the list of options short and simple.

8. **Use the five-point scale:** The five-point scale (see pages 37-38) is very useful for prioritizing and getting perspective. What's more important? What should I care about the most? What's the most risky? The most time-constrained? Use a five-point rating scale to help your grandchild become more skilled at weighing options.

9. **Play noticing games:** If your grandchild is young, you can help her develop more focus by playing noticing games such as *I Spy.* Instead of limiting the game to colors, challenge your grandchild to assess her surroundings: *"I spy ... something that could be dangerous if someone were bouncing a ball in here. I spy ... something that hasn't been put away. I spy ... something that's breakable."*

10. **Develop a special signal for getting the child's attention in public:** Be prepared to handle inappropriate actions in public. Your signal could be a word, a phrase, or a gesture. When you give the signal, the child is to come over to you and hold your hand, if appropriate for the child's age. Rehearse using the signal at home ahead of time. Role-play it to help it stick, but don't be too surprised if he doesn't follow it the first few times. In time, he'll get it.

Further, ask the child to create a signal to use when he's feeling scared or uncomfortable and wants to leave. Practice this signal at home so that you're used to noticing it. When he uses the signal, respond immediately by helping him escape the situation.

Maria decided to take charge of the situation. Dean needed to get his computer games in his backpack before his mother arrived to pick him up. But clearly he couldn't do it on his own.

"I'm setting a timer, Dean," she said, getting the electronic timer from the kitchen. She spun the dial. "Do you think you can put these games in your backpack within three minutes?"

Dean shrugged. "Sure."

"Okay. Start ... now!"

Maria watched. Dean grabbed one item after another and shoved it in the bag. He zipped up his backpack with two minutes to spare.

"Super!" Maria said with a smile. "Now you need to do three more things." She grabbed a pen and paper. "You need to brush your teeth, put on your shoes, and put on your hat." She wrote the three items in a checklist format. Then she handed him the paper and pen. "Check them off as you get them done. Do you want me to time you?"

Dean nodded. "My last time was five minutes. I think I can beat that time."

"I think you can, too," Maria said. "If you do it, you can bring home half the cookies we baked this afternoon." She reset the timer. "Are you ready? Start ... now!"

Chapter 6
Grandma's House, Grandma's Rules: Controlling Behavior

Anna plopped onto the sofa. "I give up."

"What's going on?" her husband, Vinh, asked.

"Ariel won't do anything I tell her. She ignores every rule."

"What have you tried?"

"I've tried telling her that if she didn't follow the rules, I'd take her computer privileges away. And I did. But that didn't make her follow the rules. Instead, she spent a half-hour wailing at me that I'm a thief and a bully and that she was going to report me to her mother."

Vinh winced. "I've had the same kinds of problems. I ask her to put things away, and it's as if she didn't even hear me. I feel like a ghost."

At your house, people should have to follow your rules. No-body wants to live in chaos. But because of their challenges, children with ASD can be difficult to pull in line. It can be like trying to herd cats.

Examples of Misunderstandings About Discipline	
You ...	**Your Grandchild ...**
• assume he knows you're the boss	• is unaware of roles such as "boss"
• assume he wants to please you	• isn't aware that you want to be pleased
• don't like backtalk and insolence from a child	• laughs, grins, and blurts things out at inappropriate times
• feel a responsibility to guide him through his day	• lives in his own world, not yours
• believe your punishments are reasonable	• believes you're bullying him when you tell him what to do
• believe he should apologize for hitting his brother	• feels justified in hitting his brother because he was just getting him back
• assume telling him to do something is enough	• didn't even hear you

All children test boundaries; children with ASD are no different. Avoid letting guilt or pity guide your thinking. Firm rules and schedules make children feel more secure, provided they're enforced in a helpful way. As a general rule, for best results, focus on teaching your grandchild, raising his awareness of the need for rules and order, and organizing his thoughts, rather than on punishing.

Above all, present a united front. Grandma and Grandpa should apply the rules the same way all the time.

> **How Come He Doesn't Do What I Tell Him to Do?**
>
> There are many possible reasons:
>
> - His brain may not be processing what he hears (see Chapter 2).
> - He may have decided that you're interrupting him, so you'll just have to wait until he's ready.
> - He may have decided that it's more reasonable for him to continue his activity than do what you want him to do.
> - He doesn't agree with you, and he assumes you know what he thinks.
> - He forgot what you said a few seconds after you said it.

Finding a Discipline Method That Works

1. **Beware of the limitations of traditional discipline methods:**
    The traditional, "tried and true" methods of disciplining children have a way of backfiring with children with ASD. Most traditional discipline methods don't make much sense – a fatal weakness for disciplining these kids. For example, you might say, *"Joel, stop kicking your sister under the table or I'll send you away from the table!"* But Joel is kicking his sister because he's having a hard time sitting still, he hates the food, and he's bored. Your "promise" of sending him away from the table sounds like a great deal. So, of course, he'll kick his sister again.

> **How to Respond to Friends Who Say, "You're Spoiling Her!"**
>
> "She's taking advantage of you. She's talking back to you. She's got you wrapped around her little finger."
>
> There's no end to the advice out there about how to discipline your grandchildren. Most people who don't know about ASD attribute all the behaviors to poor parenting. Don't judge them too harshly – they just don't know. Instead say, "I've set limits for her. But she's got her own limits, too. That's the way it works in our relationship – we both have to accept each other's limits. Besides, sometimes a grandma gets to spoil her grandchild."

2. **Beware of the consequences of giving consequences:** Children with ASD don't learn especially well from consequences. They get caught up in the injustice of a consequence, especially if it doesn't have anything to do with the offense (for example, losing computer time for hitting his sister), and lose the point entirely. However, consequences that match the offense (for example, losing computer time for misusing computer privileges) can work, provided your grandchild understands the connection. Post the rule and the consequence in advance.

3. **Avoid returning fire for fire:** If you feel your grandchild is being disrespectful of you, avoid the temptation to return the "disrespect" to "show" him. He won't make the connection, and you'll end up looking like a bully in his eyes.

4. **Give choices:** Choice allows your grandchild to feel she has some control. (*"Do you want to put this away right now, or in five minutes on the timer?"*) Don't offer wiggle room, just choices within the limits.

5. **Be prepared to apologize or negotiate:** If you lose your temper, apologize later. Explain how you were feeling and get the child to explain how she was feeling, so that you can decide together how you can do things differently to avoid these kinds of problems. This may feel like "giving in" to her, but it's not. It's respectful, and it models how to repair relationship problems.

6. **Be consistent:** Say what you mean, and mean what you say. Don't say something if you're not planning to follow through on it.

7. **Consider the other siblings:** It's hard to have different sets of rules for different children. A jealous sibling may accuse you of playing favorites. Sit down with a sibling and explain the benefits of some separate rules for the sibling with ASD. You may also ask for tips on what works at home.

8. **Let go of the last word:** Many children with ASD grab the last word. If you grab it at the same time, the discipline episode never ends. So let your grandchild have the last word. You get the last

action, which is far more important. Remember: Your goal was to improve the child's behavior, not to win a war of words.

9. **Choose your battles:** Your household can handle only one inflexible person, not two. As the adult, you're the one who has to adapt. A grandparent who insists on things being done her way will face a long day of meltdowns. It's not worth it. Instead, choose your battles. Some issues can wait for another day. Your goal is to make your time together enjoyable, not perfect. Sometimes the right thing to do is to just let it go.

Helping Your Grandchild Hear You

All young children have difficulties listening, but your grandchild has unique challenges. His ears can hear just fine; the way his brain processes the information doesn't always work smoothly. As a result, it can seem as if he's deaf or deliberately not paying attention.

Strategies to Help Your Grandchild Focus on What You're Saying

1. **Ask him to repeat what you just said:** If the child merely parrots back your words (like an echo), ask a few questions to make sure his brain in engaged.

2. **Draw a stick man picture:** This may seem excessive, but a picture *is* worth a thousand words. A child who has difficulty making sense of spoken words is often able to understand them when attached to pictures. Make sure your grandchild is looking at the pictures as you draw them as the movement of your hand drawing helps understanding for a visual learner. (Note: Nothing elaborate is required here.)

3. **Keep instructions simple:** Give only one task at a time. Many children with ASD have difficulty with auditory memory, which means it is hard for them to retain what they hear. As a result, they can't remember a series of instructions. Writing everything down is also helpful, if appropriate.

4. **Use clear and precise words:** *"Clean up the mess in the hallway"* may seem clear to you, but it doesn't spell out exactly what you want your grandchild to do. Instead, say *Put your shoes in the closet. Now hang up your coat on the coat-hook. Now carry your backpack to your room.* By using nouns he can see *(shoes, closet, coat, coat-hook, backpack, room)* rather than abstract words *(clean, mess)*, you make your instructions easier to follow.

5. **Phrase your instructions in positives, not negatives:** Say, *"Put the stick down"* rather than *"Don't hit your brother with that stick."* (He may just get another stick, he may start hitting the dog, etc.)

The Ten-Minute Tidy-Up[8]

Your grandchild likely has a hard time cleaning up. Messes can seem overwhelming. She won't even know where to begin or how to tackle it.

You can simplify the chore of cleaning with a timer. Set it to ten minutes. Explain to the child that it's a race to put as many things away as you can in the ten minutes. Once the timer stops, everyone stops, even if there are still a few things lying around. You're done. That's clean enough.

Three Popular Discipline Methods

Here are three discipline methods used by ASD families. None of them works all the time, but each provides a starting point.

The 1–2–3 Method[9]

How it works: When you ask your grandchild to do something (or stop doing something) and she isn't complying, say "That's 1." If she persists, say "That's 2." If she still persists, say "That's 3" and give

---

8 The Ten-Minute Tidy-Up is a clean-up technique in *Comic Sense* (2010) by Nancy Mucklow. It removes the open-endedness of clean-up activities by setting a clear time limit.

9 Based on the 1-2-3 Magic method developed by Dr. Thomas Phelan, Parent Magic Inc. Many public libraries carry the 1-2-3 Magic video series.

her the consequence. The 1-2-3 method gives the child two chances to choose to comply. The simple words cut through any confusion and focus her attention on the fact that a consequence is imminent. Most children learn to act as soon as you count to 1. To be effective, the 1-2-3 method must be delivered in a calm, unemotional voice. You also need to explain the 1-2-3 method and set up the consequences in advance so that the child knows why you're counting so that she knows what's coming if she doesn't comply.

"Derek, please put your homework away."

Derek doesn't even look away from his books.

"Derek, that's 1."

He stirred but didn't move.

"That's 2."

He looked up quickly. "What? What do I have to do?"

"Put your homework away."

He runs to do it.

Downside: The 1-2-3 method doesn't work as smoothly with ASD children as it does with other children. They don't generalize the rules from one situation to another, so they often don't know when they're doing something wrong. For some children, you have to start with "That's 2," or they'll take the extra shot. Beware of using the 1-2-3 method too much. If your grandchild ends up getting the consequences most of the time, it will confuse her and teach her that she can never succeed.

Rewards

How it works: A reward is not a bribe! Bribes are gifts or payments that manipulate or influence a child to do something immoral or unethical. Rewards are prizes for behaving in a desirable way *after* the child has behaved properly. Set up a chart with all the tasks or behaviors you need the child to comply with. Negotiate together a reward for each one or for the whole set, and write the rewards down on the chart. Now your demands are predictable and knowable. Help your grandchild focus on the chart so that he can achieve his rewards. Most important, be sure to pay up every time.

Downside: Providing rewards all the time can get wearisome (and expensive). Keep the rewards small and simple. Plan on phasing them out when the child reaches a certain age.

Token Economies

How it works: Use stickers, stars, or coins as tokens. Create a chart or set up a jar for the tokens your grandchild receives for complying with tasks and behaviors. Subtract or remove tokens for not complying. He can use the tokens to buy prizes.

Downside: Token economies are complicated to set up, and they tend to lose steam after a while. But they work in the short term, which may be enough to get some behaviors turned around. In addition, some children get fixated on the tokens, especially when they lose tokens, and lose sight of the behaviors you're trying to change.

Instead of physical tokens, consider creating a reward book. Set it up like a bank account, with credits and debits. When the child reaches a certain "balance," he can cash it in for a reward. But be prepared: Your grandchild may demand that you have a reward book, too. After all, relationship costs and benefits go both ways.

Final Note: Dealing With Extreme Behavior

Many, many children with ASD are completely unaggressive. However, some can't control their anger. There's always a chance they can hurt their siblings, damage objects, or hurt you. On occasions where behavior is extreme, you need to act fast.

With a younger child, you can carry him away from the situation. If you need to avoid touching him, wrap him in his favorite blanket first. In general, it's a good idea to avoid touching an enraged child.

With an older child or teen, your options are more limited. First, get yourself and the other siblings away from the raging youth. Lock yourselves in a room if you have to, or go outside. Phone the parents and get instructions from them on how to handle the situation. If the parents aren't available, call the police. Explain that the youth has an ASD and that you can't handle him right now. Make sure that they understand that you're not pressing charges. The police will most likely have a talk with your grandchild and later with the parents to ensure a long-term solution. They may require your grandchild to get professional or medical help.

Nobody likes to do this, but safety must come first.

Anna sat down with Ariel, and together they drew up a list of the house rules. Anna then posted the list on the fridge. She explained that Ariel would have to the count of 3 to comply with the rules. For every day that she didn't have to get to "That's 2," Ariel would get a reward from the reward list.

The first week was a bit rocky. But by the second week, Ariel was used to the counting and focused quickly whenever she heard "That's 1."

Vinh, Ariel's grandpa, joined with Anna in consistently enforcing the rules. In a short time, the household became much more orderly and peaceful.

Chapter 7
Simple Language:
Bridging Communication Barriers

Abe introduced his grandson Eli to his fiancée. "Eli, this is Bina. She's going to be your step-grandmother. Bina, this is my grandson Eli."

"Nice to meet you, Eli," Bina said, extending her hand. She smiled warmly.

Eli didn't seem to notice the extended hand or the smile. He merely mumbled something incoherent and turned away.

Abe followed him. "Eli, that was rude," he whispered. "Bina was trying to make a nice first contact, and you just walked away."

"I didn't say anything bad," Eli answered matter-of-factly.

"But you just walked away. You didn't shake her hand. That makes her feel as if you don't want to meet her."

"I didn't know I was supposed to."

"Do you think you could go back and try again?"

Eli walked back over to Bina, grabbed her hand, and pumped it a couple of times. "There. I shook your hand. Now here's everything about me. I like computers and computer games. My favorite games are ..."

Then Eli launched into a long monologue about all his interests, his gaze drifting around the room while he talked.

Communication means more than just words. Body language, facial expressions, gaze, voice, and gestures are as important to a message as words are. Yet, children with ASD don't naturally use non-verbal communication, and they don't understand it when they see it. As a result, they frequently miscommunicate and misunderstand.

Most children with ASD have at least some of the following communication challenges.

Common Communication Challenges in Children With ASD	
Cause	**Communication Challenges**
Weak executive function	• Finding the words they want to use • Controlling emotions (e.g., suddenly laughing or crying at inappropriate times) • Organizing communication (e.g., forgetting what they're talking about, or not having a plan)
Disconnect between emotions and logic	• Communicating emotion with voice, face, or body language • Reading body language • Identifying the emotions of others (besides happy and sad) • Identifying their own emotions
Weak theory of mind	• Including important details that the listener doesn't know • Knowing when their listeners are bored or angry • Being polite, tactful, and empathetic • Understanding that some thoughts are not for sharing
Weak relationship skills	• Managing the give-and-take of conversation • Using conversation to deepen a relationship or get to know someone • Remembering to greet friends and use polite manners
Rigidity	• Accepting interruptions without needing to start over • Following topic changes

Miscommunicating

Miscommunicating means communicating a message that's different from what you intended. Your grandchild may inadvertently send the wrong message because she chooses the wrong words or expresses herself poorly with her body language. Her communication may also appear tactless, communicating disdain instead of the respect and affection she actually feels.

The counselor looked at Amrita and smiled. "Would you like to take French next year?"

"Nope," Amrita answered flatly.

"Oh." The counselor was taken aback. "Well, how about another language?"

"I don't like languages. They're stupid. We can all get by with just English. Everybody speaks English."

The counselor put down her pen and gave Amrita a long look. After a long moment, Amrita asked, "Is there something wrong with your eyes?"

"Are you being sarcastic with me?" the counselor said very slowly.

"No," Amrita said. And she stood up and walked out of the room.

It may take your grandchild a long time to learn to communicate effectively. She may already be in special programs and classes, and her parents may be working on communication skills at home, so there's no need to pile on more "programming" at your house. Accept that her communication is incomplete and find little ways to help her communicate more effectively with you.

Above all, avoid correcting her all the time. Occasional tips are useful, but constant advice is too much like badgering and may make the child reluctant to talk at all.

Misunderstanding

You may already have noticed that your grandchild easily misunderstands what you say to him. If he's listening to your words, he may not be reading your body language or listening for your feelings, wants, intentions, and unspoken messages.

Here are some of the misunderstandings you're likely to notice.

1. **Misreading your intentions:** The child may believe you're angry simply because you're offering advice. He may get offended when you're just being helpful. He can't see your intentions, even if you try to show your goodwill through facial expressions.

2. **Understanding too literally:** Children with ASD tend to take words very literally. This is a disadvantage because other people rarely put their thoughts precisely into words. They use vague or approximate wording and expect others to know what they mean.

"Jesse, I told you to put on your shoes!" Wilhelm said sternly.

"But I don't have any shoes."

Wilhelm picked up the footwear and pressed them into Jesse's hands. "These!"

"But those are boots," Jesse said in confusion.

"You know what I meant!"

Your grandchild may also have difficulty with figurative expressions and sayings. He may get caught up in the literal meaning of the words and can't understand how the expression works.

"Sorry, Ana," Marta said wearily. "I don't feel like talking. I have a load on my mind."

Ana stared at the top of Marta's head. Then she frowned. "Where?"

Why Does He Get Upset Over Teasing?

Most children with ASD don't know how to handle teasing. They can't read the intentions of the other person, so they assume all teasing is malicious. They don't understand that teasing is often playful and friendly.

Your grandchild may accuse you of teasing her. Perhaps you were teasing, but in a good way. Help her understand by explaining your intentions. If she's still offended, offer her a chance to practice teasing you. Make sure she includes friendly body language such as smiling or winking.

Quick Tips

1. **Address him by name:** Instead of *"Please pass me a napkin,"* say, *"Paul, please pass me a napkin."* Otherwise, your grandchild might not understand that you're speaking to him.

2. **Have a "stop" signal:** Many children with ASD don't know when to stop talking. By stoically enduring an endless monologue, you are not helping him learn about two-way communication. Instead, develop a signal to use when you want him to wrap it up, or simply state: *"That's enough on that topic for today."*

3. **Avoid sarcasm (use of false, mocking praise and verbal irony):** Your grandchild will likely take you very, very literally.

   Todd came running into the house in his new white sweater, his hands covered in car grease.

   "What on earth were you doing playing outside in your new clothes?" Mary asked, hands on her hips.

   Todd looked at his hands, then back to his grandmother in confusion. "I was playing with dad's car." He showed her his hands.

Mary gritted her teeth. "And I suppose now you're going to wipe those greasy hands on your nice, new white sweater!" she said sarcastically.

And so he did!

4. **Limit repetition:** Some children with ASD ask the same question over and over again, as if they're stuck in a loop. Write the answer on a card. When she asks her question again, simply point to the answer card instead of answering.

5. **Set a time every day when the child can talk to you about her special interest:** Your grandchild delights in talking about her special interest, but your patience has limits. Add a special interest discussion time on the schedule with a set time limit. If she brings up the subject at another time, refer her to the schedule. Then during the scheduled time, give her your full attention.

6. **Develop a formula for initiating communication:** Your grandchild may have a habit of just launching into a monologue. By accepting this behavior, you're not doing him any favors. You can gently teach him how to properly initiate communication:

   Luis bounded into the room, grabbed his grandfather, and immediately started talking. "You go to the store for me today to get me some more batteries and ..."

   "Hold it," his grandfather said, holding up a hand. "That's not how I showed you to start a conversation with me. You're supposed to say 'Grandpa?' Then you wait for me to look at you. When I say 'Yes?' you can start talking to me. Then you'll have my attention and my permission to talk. Let's try again, shall we?"

> **Standing too Close and Staring**
>
> Some children with ASD stand too close when they talk to others. Since they're not in the habit of searching for body language, they don't see a need to look at the whole person. Advise your grandchild to stand back far enough to be able to see the other person from the waist up while looking at the face.
>
> Some children stare instead of making natural eye contact. Sometimes it just means they're lost in their own world. They're not really staring. At other times, they're curious about someone's face and fail to realize that the person can see them staring. Unfortunately, too many well-meaning social skills coaches tell these children to "look people in the eye," so they do so very literally. If you grandchild stares, ask her why. If she's staring in an effort to make eye contact, explain that eye contact means glancing at the face to read facial expressions, not staring at the person's eyeballs.

Conversation

When you're talking to someone, you're probably not aware of all the "conversation work" you're doing. You watch the other person's face and body language to gauge his or her reactions. You smooth over misunderstandings, give subtle feedback, and adapt what you say to what the other person seems to be interested in. Basically, you do a lot of work to keep the conversation going.

Here are some examples of conversation work that you probably do without realizing you're doing it.

- **Observing:** Watching body language or listening to tone of voice to stay aware of your listener's emotions, intentions, or interest.

- **Repairing:** Fixing mistakes by apologizing or withdrawing a comment (for example, *"I'm sorry that I blurted that out. Please disregard what I just said."*).

- **Mirroring:** Reflecting back what the other person said to show interest and acknowledge his or her feelings (for example, "*It must have been hard to live through war times like that.*").

- **Listening:** Actively thinking about what the other person is saying.

- **Following:** Adapting to the flow of topics without trying to backtrack to a topic of interest.

- **Encouraging:** Interjecting comments and facial signals of interest and encouragement to let the speaker know you're listening (for example, "*Wow. Really? That's interesting.*").

- **Sharing control:** Allowing everyone an equal share of control of the conversation and resisting the urge to interrupt or argue.

Children with ASD have difficulty with the give-and-take of conversation and often fail to do the little things that keep conversation going.

Quick Tips

1. **Accept your grandchild's limitations:** Conversation is about people, not about words. Your goal in talking together is to enjoy being with each other. So above all, find ways to make conversation fun.

2. **Keep conversations balanced:** Avoid the temptation to let your grandchild control your conversations. He needs to learn that everyone in a conversation is equal. Gently insist on your turn to speak and his turn to listen.

3. **Help the child learn the unwritten rules:** Raise your expectations for the child's conversation skills as he gets more experience. Here are some rules you can help him learn:

   - **Don't hog the conversation.** Avoid saying more than one or two sentences at a time. Wait for the other person's response.

- **Check the listeners' faces.** See if you have permission to continue talking. If the listener looks bored or ready to jump in and say something, then stop talking.

- **Link your contributions to the last thing that was said.** You can't backtrack to an old topic.

- **Ask questions instead of lecturing.** Use questions to discover interesting things about people, but avoid asking personal questions about money, sexuality, weight, health, or private relationships. Also avoid asking questions to which the answer is obvious (for example, *Is your shirt red?*).

- **Accept interruptions.** If the person is responding to your comment before you finish, then he/she has jumped in because of enthusiasm, not boredom. Just smile and say "Yeah."

- **Learn people's names.** Using someone's name makes them feel good. It's a way of showing respect.

- **Avoid repeating yourself.** To avoid saying something twice, stop thinking about it. Think about something else.

- **Smile to show warmth and acceptance.** But stop smiling when someone starts talking about sad news.

Abe watched as his fiancée Bina listened to Eli's monologue. He sighed. Perhaps he should have spent more time preparing him for meeting her.

"Eli," Bina interrupted in a gentle voice, "you've told me a lot about your meteorology hobby. And I'm fascinated, because I watch the weather on TV every day. But why don't we give me a turn to talk?"

Eli gave her an odd look. "Why?"

"So that you can learn what kind of person I am and what kind of grandma I'm going to be," she said without missing a beat.

"Step-grandma."

"Right. Step-grandma. So ... what do you want to know? What about the kinds of things I like to bake?"

"You bake things?" Eli was looking interested.

"Mostly cookies, but sometimes brownies. What sorts of baking do you like?"

Abe listened in utter amazement as Bina drew Eli into a real conversation.

Chapter 8
Education: Learning Beyond School

Rosita watched her ten-year-old grandson Marcos draw a picture. Not surprisingly, it was a picture of a chemistry lab, the exact same chemistry lab he'd been drawing for the past year.

She was amazed at the detail he produced. Clearly, he understood the experiment that he was drawing, but she'd seen him draw this exact picture at least thirty times.

Didn't he ever get bored of drawing it? Was he somehow learning something by doing it over and over? Or was he stuck?

On previous occasions, he'd seemed much more absorbed. Today he seemed as if he was doing it quickly, just to get it out of the way.

Rosita wondered if he'd still be drawing the same picture a year from now.

Learning Styles

For children with ASD, learning fact- and logic-based material comes easy. The hard part is learning about people, motives, and the social world. Here are some of the more common learning traits in children with ASD.

ASD and Learning	
General Trait	**Typical Behaviors**
Average or above-average intelligence	• Learns quickly • Tends to have high grades in favorite subjects • Can have an extremely high IQ
Impressive memory for facts	• Good memorization skills • Likes trivial details • Likes fact- and logic-based careers (science, technology, computers)
Precocious learners	• Learns math or reading at a very young age • Teaches himself the skills he wants to learn
Creativity and originality	• Has a unique way of thinking and feeling • Is capable of very original thought • Is often involved in the arts (drama, music, art)
Ability to microfocus	• Can withdraw completely from the world and focus on his work • May be able to hold and manipulate 3D objects in her mind

Rosita remembered how, at age two, Marcos was interested in pouring liquids together to watch them blend. He was forever stirring, mixing, and shaking concoctions. He also liked to open containers in the kitchen and spill the contents on the floor to study them.

By age two and a half, he could read. He could talk too, but he still hadn't learned to call anyone by name, not even "Mama" or "Dada."

It was hard to figure out how chemistry came so easily to such a young child. Rosita had spent hours trying to teach him to build towers of blocks or play cars, but he wasn't interested in anything she thought he should learn.

By the time he was ready for kindergarten, Marcos was already reading at a mid-elementary level yet couldn't understand basic storylines in children's books.

Repetition: A Learning Style or Perseveration?

Children with ASD tend to do the same thing over and over again – drawing the same picture, playing the same tune on the piano, or watching the same video. The sameness helps them feel safe in an otherwise confusing world of change.

Do these children learn anything through all this repetition? Oddly enough, many do. While you may not notice it, your grandchild's understanding of the activity deepens with each repetition. Her style changes. She experiments a little. Over time, she adds, embellishes, and streamlines her work.

It may drive you bonkers, but it's not doing any harm. However, watch for signs that the child is stuck and doesn't know how to move on. For example, if she always draws the same picture, today she might draw it quickly and messily and seem unhappy when it's done. Find light and nonintrusive ways to pique her interest in new activities. For example, you could suggest some new objects to add to her favorite picture and then draw along with her to make it a shared activity. Or you could suggest new things to draw.

What Is Synesthesia?

Synesthesia is a neurological difference that causes the person's sensory or thinking pathways to blend in particular ways. In the most common types of synesthesia, the person experiences letters or numbers as colors or shapes. However, others can hear their sense of motion, picture time in terms of shapes or maps, or envision days of the week as personalities.

Synesthesia is extremely rare. But it is less rare in people on the autism spectrum than in the rest of the population.

School

School is a high-stress environment for many children with ASD. Classes in reading, math, and other traditional subjects may strike the child as boring and redundant, because he already taught himself these subjects through reading. Yet, the classes he'd really need, such as social skills, emotional skills, coordination, and friendship building, are hard to find. Meanwhile, unstructured big-group playtime, such as recess, is difficult for a child who gets confused in social situations.

Typical School Stressors

- Constant noise
- Frequent and abrupt transitions
- Competitiveness
- Group projects
- Recess
- Lunch time
- Gym class
- Sitting still

- Lack of quiet or alone time
- Handwriting
- Initiating and completing tasks
- Processing complex verbal instructions
- Boredom
- Bullies and unfriendly peers
- Lack of friends

Stress for the Whole Family

At the end of the day, your grandchild brings all this school stress home. Parents deal with the phone calls from the principal; meetings with confused teachers; and detentions, suspensions, and other punishments. Many children with ASD receive special education services in their school. Some parents end up placing their child in a private school. If the new school is a good fit, it might be worth the money. Other parents pull their children out of school and teach them at home.

All of this means that the family can carry as much stress as your grandchild. Offering a sympathetic ear, supporting their schooling efforts in any way you can, and providing a stress-free, comfortable place for your grandchild are ways you can help out.

What Is Special Education?

Special education is any programming targeted at the specific needs of specific children. Special education programs are usually offered in the regular school system. Your grandchild's classroom may have a part-time aide who helps her and other children stay organized and focused and navigates her through the school day. Or she may attend one or more special classes once or twice a week or sometimes every school day.

Examples of Special Education Programs

- **Social skills classes:** Special programs that teach social interaction skills

- **Remedial classes:** School-based extra-help programs for children with low achievement

- **Tutoring programs:** Extra-help programs. Often these are private, paid for by the parents

- **Occupational therapy:** Programs run by occupational therapists, often related to sensory issues and learning how to be calm and relaxed

- **Applied behavioral analysis (ABA):** A set of interventions that teach new skills using demonstrations, reinforcement, practice opportunities and so forth

- **Speech and language services:** Professional programs to help children who have social, speech, and communication difficulties

- **Other:** Special summer camps, fitness programs, and swimming lessons

Special Education Jargon

ADHD: Children with attention deficit hyperactivity disorder have difficulty focusing, paying attention, remembering, or sitting still. Some children with ASD have ADHD as well.

Exceptional student: Usually the term "exceptional student" refers to children who have physical or developmental disabilities. But in some districts, it also refers to any student who has an IEP and needs special programming, including gifted and talented students (see below).

Gifted and talented: A gifted or talented student is a child who has been tested and found to have an unusual or exceptional ability to learn in one or several areas, such as math, science, art, music, drama, sports, or general creativity. As a result, the child needs programming not usually provided by the school. The child may or may not have high grades.

IEP: An Individualized Education Program (IEP) is a school document that spells out what special education services a child will receive and why. It provides goals, strategies, assessment procedures, and any other information to help the school provide for the child.

Learning disability: A learning disability is a disorder that affects learning in special areas (such as reading or math). In unimpacted areas, the child usually demonstrates at least average abilities. Learning disabilities include difficulties with reading, doing math, writing, using language, or understanding spoken language.

Suspension: A suspension is a school punishment that sends the child home for one to three days. An "in-school" suspension requires the child to sit in a separate detention room at school, and is less severe than a regular suspension.

Zero tolerance: Zero tolerance is a school policy of automatically punishing children for serious infractions of school rules, with no consideration of the child's knowledge and ability, the circumstances, or other context factors. Although popular for a while, zero tolerance policies are becoming less common in schools.

Homeschooling

Homeschooling means taking a child out of a public or private school system and teaching her at home. A parent has to provide all the instruction and learning opportunities. Some families also explore "un-schooling," which means providing a rich learning environment and letting the child learn through play, game play, household responsibilities, work experience, and social interaction. Laws and rules governing home-schooling and unschooling vary across states.

Homeschooling and unschooling were very unusual just a few decades ago, but now many families choose these alternatives. Each family has their own reasons for teaching their child at home. For example, home is a calm, peaceful place for children with ASD, whereas school is a high-stress place. Learning can often take place more easily at home.

Avoid assuming that the homeschooled child isn't getting an education. Support the parents in their decision to provide one-on-one education to your grandchild.

How long will a child get homeschooled? Most of the time, homeschooling focuses on the elementary school years. Many parents are reluctant to try to teach high school subjects, and many young teens are eager to try out school. However, some teens with ASD take courses over the Internet and finish their high school diploma at home.

After School at Grandma's House

In families where both parents have jobs, a grandchild may go to grandma's house for an hour or two after school. If your grandchild comes to your house every afternoon during the school week, you've probably already developed some strategies for dealing with the after-school hours.

You may have noticed that your grandchild comes home most days in an agitated state. He may even burst into tears each and every day. He's upset by something that happened on the bus, confused by the actions of other children, or worried about homework. But more than anything else, he's just worn out and at the end of his tether. It's been a hard day. He needs to let go.

Helping Your Grandchild Decompress

Here are some ideas for helping your grandchild shake off the stress of school.

1. **Mouth tools:** Mouth tools (see Chapter 2) are soothing and help get rid of any wound-up or wound-down feelings. A few minutes of chewing, sucking, crunching, or blowing can wash away a day of stress.

2. **Muscle play:** For many children with ASD, trampoline-bouncing, jumping, crashing, or rolling in the marshmallow bag (see Chapter 2) wake up the senses and make the body feel whole and good again.

3. **Reading alone:** Maybe your grandchild just needs to be by herself. She doesn't want anyone to talk to her until she's had an hour alone. Give her the space she needs in a safe environment.

4. **Sensory stimulation:** A grandchild who craves smells or textures (see Chapter 2) may want to spend an hour doing nothing else except smelling pleasant smells or petting the cat. Quiet sensory activities are very soothing.

What to Avoid

1. **Chores:** Your grandchild isn't ready to work on chores right away after school. School can be very stressful, so allow the child some down time before prompting him about chores.

2. **Homework:** Having to sit still, struggling to write, and focusing on work he's not interested in are the very reasons why he's in a bad state. So leave homework till later.

3. **Lectures or long talks:** When your grandchild is in an agitated or wound-down state, he can't hear you. Lectures and long discussions are pointless. Wait until he's feeling calm again.

4. **Changes and surprises:** After-school routines are essential for making the transition from school to home as calm as possible. Together with the parents and the child, decide on an after-school routine at your house. If you have to change it occasionally, give the family advance notice so that the child is aware of the change to prevent unpleasant surprises.

What Is Bullying?

Bullying is a power tactic. Children who bully say or do things specifically to make another child miserable. Bullying can include calling names, saying or writing nasty things, excluding someone from activities, threatening, making someone feel uncomfortable or scared, taking or damaging their things, or making them do things they don't want to do.

Children with ASD are often the targets of bullies, partly because they don't "blend in," they have difficulty with communication and social skills, and they usually don't have many friends to protect and stand up for them. Schools have become much more vigilant about bullying, but there's still a long way to go.

If your grandchild tells you tales about bullying at school, listen. Ask questions to help him fill in the details. Later, pass on the information to the parents in case they need to call the school to follow up.

Be aware that sometimes children with ASD believe they're being bullied when they aren't. Since they can't read body language, they can't determine the other child's intent. They may assume that if someone says "no" or bumps into them, that's bullying. You grandchild may even decide that everything people do that she doesn't like is bullying.

You can help your grandchild get perspective on bullying by asking questions. *What was the person doing? What did his facial expression look like? Was he laughing? Do you think he was trying to scare you or force you to do things?* Help your grandchild pull all the facts together so that he can determine the person's motive.

Some kids with ASD are so anxious to have friends and receive social attention that they put up with behaviors that would normally be classified as bullying. Again, listen carefully when your grandchild talks about other kids, school, etc.

Handling Homework

If you live in an extended family household, or you keep your grandchild till after supper, it may fall to you to help him with his homework. Here are some tips for success with homework.

1. **Develop daily homework routines:** Make sure "homework" is written into the schedule and gets an adequate block of time. Avoid changing the homework time. But keep in mind that your grandchild may need some relaxation time before starting homework.

2. **Clear away clutter:** Many children with ASD are distractible. Provide a clean table or desk in an uncluttered, quiet room for the child to work in so she can better concentrate.

3. **Beware of misunderstandings:** Your grandchild may misunderstand the teacher's instructions, especially if they were given verbally and not written down. You may have to assess the homework yourself to determine if his understanding makes sense.

Rayyan checked up on Amar to make sure he was reading the assigned novel.

"Hey, great job, Amar! You're already in the middle of the book!"

Amar grinned and nodded as she sat down beside him.

"So, Amar, can you tell me what's happened so far?"

Amar frowned. "What do you mean 'what's happened so far'?"

"I mean since the beginning of the book," Rayyan explained.

He looked confused. "But I haven't read the beginning of the book."

"Then how can you be in the middle of the book?"

"I just opened it there. I've read a few other parts, too."

"But you haven't been reading the pages in order?"

"The teacher didn't say to read the book in order. She just said to read it."

4. **Have phone numbers of classmates handy:** Being able to phone a classmate to ask for instructions that your grandchild misunderstood, copied wrong, or left at school is a homework lifesaver. As well, some school districts have homework hotlines and telephone tutors that you can call when you don't understand the homework. Ask the parents what free homework help is available in your area.

5. **Provide sensory accommodations:** If your grandchild is bouncy, let him sit on a yoga ball to do homework. If his handwriting is awkward, let him type it on the computer, provided his teacher and parents have approved. If he loses focus quickly, let him have a minute on the trampoline after every three questions. Provide the accommodations he needs.

6. **Don't overdo it:** When hours have passed, homework has become stressful, and concentration is foggy, it may be time to pack it in. There's not much point in forcing the child to sit in agony longer than he can concentrate. He's only learning to hate learning. Write a note to the teacher describing how much you were able to get done and why you needed to stop. Include your phone number and the parents' phone number in case the teacher needs to call you. Staple it into your grandchild's notebook so that he doesn't lose it. There may be information in the child's IEP that describes how to handle homework overload, so talk to the child's parents if you notice that homework is stressful and takes an inordinate amount of time.

Marcos was watching his favorite science show. Rosita sat down beside him and tried to follow the show. It was interesting – all about new discoveries in chemistry.

Marcos was completely engrossed in the show and didn't seem to notice that Rosita had joined him. But during commercials, he pulled his eyes away from the TV.

"Hi, Marcos," Rosita said quietly during the first commercial break. "I'm going to watch the show, too. What did I miss at the beginning?"

Marcos looked surprised. But his eyes brightened, and he promptly filled her in. Rosita kept an eye on the TV and alerted him when the commercials were winding down. He stopped talking instantly and refocused on the show.

At every commercial, they chatted. Rosita asked questions, and Marcos answered. The time limits were built in, since the commercials were always over within a couple of minutes.

By the end of the show, Rosita decided that the interactions were so successful she'd watch with him every week. She asked him for a book to read in the meantime so that she could catch up to his knowledge.

Chapter 9
Matriarch, Patriarch:
Leading the Family Into Acceptance

"Happy Thanksgiving, Mom!" Leah said, giving Kathryn a hug as soon as she answered the door. "Here, I brought the mashed potatoes and the apple pie."

"Hi, Denis," Kathryn said to her nine-year-old grandson who was standing behind his mother, not making eye contact but clutching a book.

"Mm-hm, hi," Denis replied, and then maneuvered his way around his mother and grandmother and walked into the living room.

"Hey! It's Denis!" his uncle William roared with a grin. Denis winced and backed up. "I haven't seen you in ages, boy!" William walked over and gave Denis a slap on the back.

"Ow!" Denis yelled, outraged. "You hit me! You're mean! Don't ever do that to me again!"

"Hey! Touchy kid! I was just saying hi!" William glared at his sister-in-law. "Teach him some manners, will ya?"

"William ..." Leah started, trying to intervene, but he'd already sniffed and stalked off.

Denis stood smoldering in the middle of the living room. His young cousin Ted stared at him for a long moment, then started to giggle.

At that, Denis lost control. He screamed, threw his book at Ted, then shoved past his mother and ran outside.

"Denis!"

Leah ran after him. Kathryn followed.

They found him several minutes later in the back seat of the car under a blanket. They tried to persuade him to come back inside.

"Go away" was all he'd say.

Kathryn sighed. So much for a happy Thanksgiving!

As matriarchs and patriarchs of the family, grandparents play a unique role in the extended family life of a grandchild with ASD. Most of your grandchild's relatives have very little understanding of his challenges and differences. One of your jobs is to help educate the whole family so that the child feels comfortable among them.

Big family events should be occasions for closeness and enjoyment. But holidays are never like the ones on television when one of the children has an ASD. If the family isn't properly prepared, it could be a disaster.

Family Gatherings

What's stressful about a big family event for a child with ASD?

- **Lack of predictability:** It's a big upset to her routines. She out of her "normal" life and her safety zone.

- **Sensory overload:** She's being bombarded by new sounds, smells, and sensations.

- **Fears:** She's dealing with people who don't accommodate to her, usually several all at once.

- **Relatives:** They talk too loud, get too close, or touch without permission.

- **Food:** She may expect to hate the meal, so she resents being dragged to the event.

Because she's anxious and uncomfortable, anything can set her off. Being aware of this is the first step toward making your family event successful. Basically, you'll need to prepare more than the turkey and apple pie!

You may find that sometimes the parents decline a family gathering. Don't take it personally. It may just be a bad time, or they may know it will be overwhelming for your grandchild. Set another time for a smaller gathering that they can attend so everyone will have a good time.

Quick Tips

1. **Call the parents in advance:** Ask for their suggestions for making the event go smoothly. Call again the day before the event and describe the preparations you've made to make sure you haven't misunderstood anything.

2. **Call everyone else:** Make sure everyone's aware of the child's needs, limits, and sensitivities. Ensure that relatives won't stick their face in his face, yell loud comments at him, criticize him in front of others, or touch him without permission.

3. **Provide a quiet place:** The quiet place should be a room, just for him, where there are no sharp objects, loose cords, or other hazards. Show him and the parents the room when he first arrives to be sure that it will work for him. That way, whenever he needs

to escape the noise of the family gathering, he can go there and quietly read a book, listen to soothing music, or do whatever has been found to calm him.

4. **Prepare special food for the child:** Have some of the right food on hand. He may not like to eat what everyone else eats.

5. **Prepare your grandchild ahead of time:** Describe the basic schedule for the gathering. Tell him what's on the menu so that he can choose his food in advance. Explain what you've prepared for his comfort. Tell him that he can go right to the quiet space when he first arrives if he wants – he doesn't have to jump right into the conversation. Ask if there are any other ways you can help make him comfortable.

6. **Let him do it his way:** Don't force him to join a game or outing just because everyone else does. There's no point in doing it if it'll make him miserable. His idea of fun may be very different from everyone else's.

7. **Keep the meal relaxed:** Don't worry about formalities. Keep everything light. If your grandchild prefers to eat somewhere else by himself, make him feel okay about doing that.

8. **Appreciate his efforts at table conversation:** If other family members are tired of listening to him, then you get to be his listener. Smile and be encouraging. He's trying hard!

9. **Model your expectations:** When the whole family sees how you interact with your grandchild, they are more likely to do what you do. Show them through your words and actions how to make the most of being together.

10. **Wrap it up while it's still going well:** Avoid dragging on a family event simply because no disasters have occurred yet. If the gathering goes late, and your grandchild is stuck, let him know that he can say good-bye to everyone and retreat to his quiet space.

Being Your Own Kind of Grandparent

Being the grandparent of a child with ASD is a bit like being a pioneer. You have to create your own rules and roles because the standard ones won't be a good fit. The following are examples of roles you may want to explore.

Providing Parent Respite

The common lament among parents of a child with ASD is, *"Will we ever have a normal life again?"* Loving your child doesn't mean you don't regret the loss of freedom and low-stress living. When grandparents offer to take their grandchild for an afternoon or an overnight, they contribute to the health of the marriage and the happiness of the two adults.

You may want to set realistic expectations on the limits of your offer. After all, you don't want to be babysitting every weekend. But if you can offer them an occasional evening out or weekend away, they'll be grateful.

What If You Don't Agree With What the Parents Are Doing?

It's hard to know exactly what's going on with your grandchild, especially if you don't live close by and observe things on a regular basis. There may be things happening at home and at school that you never see. So keep an open mind.

Instead of expressing skepticism about parenting methods and unfamiliar therapies, ask for information to read, such as the diagnosis report, books, or websites. Show interest, and get as much information as you can. Remember that the parents are doing this for the first time too, so your support will be much appreciated.

Some grandparents are upset if their grandchild ends up on prescription medication, but be assured that both the parents and their physician have invested a lot of time and thought in this decision. Your job is to support their decisions and help make the child's life as calm and happy as possible.

What should a grandparent do when the parents aren't facing the fact that their child has ASD? Sometimes one or both of the parents refuse to believe the diagnosis. Parents who refuse to accept a diagnosis usually just need extra time to adjust to the new reality. So talk about it without accusations or criticism. In the meantime, set up your own home to accommodate your grandchild. Until the parents ask for your input, that's all you can do while still respecting family boundaries.

Caring for Siblings

Make a point of not ignoring your other grandchildren. The brothers and sisters of a child with ASD often don't get equal time from their parents, so they'll appreciate extra attention from you. They need their own special outings and times with you.

But be aware that the siblings of children with ASD are usually rugged, realistic, and responsible little people. They've learned to roll with the punches. So don't worry about the siblings. Certainly, they need special days with their grandparents, but they don't need your pity.

Giving Gifts

You can have fun "spoiling" your grandchild with ASD with gifts. Just target his special interest. Books, magazines, toys, tools, games, and activities in his favorite subject area will always be gifts that hit the mark. For outings, go to museums and movies focusing on the same subject. These efforts will easily make you one of his favorite people.

Developing Your Own Rituals and Traditions

There's something wonderful about every child. There's also something wonderful about every family. One of a grandparent's jobs is to find those wonderful things. Your family isn't "broken" just because it doesn't match the families in the magazines, and you don't need to spend your life coping or mourning what could have been. Make the most of your time together, and build a set of family rituals and traditions that fit the family you are.

Examples of Rituals and Traditions

1. **Bedtime rituals:** Closure at the end of the day helps any child get to sleep, but especially a child with ASD. Parents may recommend certain exercises to release tension. You can help give closure by sitting on the edge of the bed and say: *"Let's talk about your day."* Avoid talking about problems or mistakes at bedtime so that you don't make the child feel anxious.

2. **Keeping a scrapbook:** Funny, enjoyable, and memorable things will happen with your grandchild. Write them down in a notebook. There may be funny stories, funny things he said or did, fun places you went, or just great conversations. This booklet will be something you can share later on.

3. **Videos:** It's fun to watch videos together as your grandchild gets older. You'll be able to see how far he's progressed.

4. **Storytelling:** All grandchildren love to hear stories about how other people made mistakes, had adventures, and made big life decisions when they were young. These stories become models for their own life's journey. If your grandchild isn't good at listening, blend your stories into her interests. For example, if she likes making videos, make videos together of your old stories. If she's interested in weather, choose stories that center around storms and heat waves.

5. **Font of wisdom:** Find opportunities to talk to teen grandchildren about the larger issues in life and the principles of good living. Parents are often too busy with programming to explore ideas such as forgiveness, apologizing, heroism, selflessness, and honor. Teach sayings and maxims, such as *A stitch in time saves nine* or make up your own maxims, such as *Words hurt, just like hitting.* The child may not learn the principles immediately, but when he's ready for them, your words will make sense.

6. **Twists on traditions:** Many children with ASD like traditions because they prefer sameness and routines. Your grandchild's rigidity will give your family enduring traditions, even if they're a bit unconventional. Don't change things if they worked last year. If the child needs to see presents before you wrap them up, then include that in your gift-giving traditions. If she refuses to eat birthday cake, create a birthday cookie. Enjoy your nontraditional traditions.

7. **Staycations:** Going away on holidays can be difficult with a child with ASD. Fill in the gap by providing entertaining *staycations.* What's nearby that the family can explore together? If your grandchild doesn't want to participate, provide an activity for the sidelines.

8. **Religious traditions:** Many children with ASD aren't able to accept a belief system. Their literalism makes them skeptical. But because they like tradition, they can still participate in re-

ligious celebrations and enjoy the sense of community. Moreover, church youth groups may be more accepting of your grandchild's differences than his peer group at school. Above all, don't express disappointment if he isn't following the "family religion." The truth is, most children choose their own path when they grow up. With a child with ASD, you just find out a little earlier.

Making Way for Happiness

"It's not that easy being green," Kermit the Frog sings. How true it is! Having different needs and perspectives from the majority of the population makes life a challenge. And yet, everyone must live the life they have, accepting themselves for who they are and learning to benefit from their differences.

Happiness is a skill, not an emotion. People have to learn the habits of happiness. You can help teach your grandchild to see his options for happiness.

1. **Build resilience:** *Resilience* means the inner strength to endure a bad time and return to happiness. No matter how hard life knocks you down, you get back up again. If you can guide your grandchild through his childhood problems, he'll develop the skills to bounce back from big ones later in life. So when problems occur, talk about ways to solve them, and help the child find a resolution.

2. **Foster a yearning for relationships:** Help your grandchild learn to want relationship skills while still young (see Chapter 4). By the teen years, she will have those skills so that she won't be lonely.

3. **Help him find his "flow":** There's a calm, sweet joy in doing the things one loves to do. The pet interest of a child with ASD brings him that kind of joy. Help him find ways to connect his interest to the outside world, through outings, books, meetings with experts, and films, so that he can learn to be happy without being isolated.

4. **Seize the day:** Fear of the shocks and discomforts of life in the wider world can hold a child with ASD back from living. Help her discover her own unique style of living.

5. **Recognize her talents:** Many experts say the future belongs to creative, original people. If that's true, then youth with ASD today have a great advantage. Show enthusiasm about your grandchild's future and find ways to support her hobbies and interests.

Overcoming Depression and Pessimism

A lot of teens with ASD have issues with depression. There are many different kinds of depression, some resulting from repeated negative life experiences, others resulting from biochemical imbalances. Support the child's family in seeking medical, social, and psychological help with depression.

In general, children with ASD tend to focus on the problems and disadvantages of everything, a pattern that paves the way for depression later on. You can help by teaching your grandchild the habit of focusing on successes, benefits, and having faith in the future.

Kathryn adjusted the ornaments on the Christmas tree as the doorbell rang. "Coming!"

It was her grandson Denis. He smiled, made brief eye contact, and handed her a bag. "Here. This is my supper."

"Thanks, Denis. Merry Christmas! Is your mom still in the car?"

"Yes." Denis walked past Kathryn. "Where's my room?"

"You can take the bedroom beside the bathroom. I put a heavy blanket in there, just like you suggested."

Denis forgot to say thank you as he went directly to the room, but Kathryn disregarded it. She was just glad that Denis and Leah arrived early so that he could settle in before the others got there.

Later that evening, Denis emerged for a while, talked briefly to his aunts and uncles, and helped the other children set the table in the dining room.

"Where do you want to eat?" Kathryn asked him quietly. "At the table with us, or at the table I set up in the kitchen?"

"I'll eat with everybody."

There was noise and commotion as everybody took a chair and helped themselves. Denis ate a selection the food items he had brought, and nobody commented on it. After ten minutes, he took his plate and left the table.

Later on, Kathryn found him in his room reading. "Thanks for eating with us, Denis. I know you find us noisy."

"Really noisy!"

"But you stayed anyway. We really like having you around and appreciate the effort you made. Is this the kind of Christmas dinner you expected after we talked on the phone yesterday?"

"A little bit." He read for a minute, then looked up. "Was it the kind of Christmas dinner you expected?"

"Yep." Kathryn gave him a little hug. "It was the best Christmas ever."

Conclusion

Ten Best Tips

1. **Always try to get a good night's sleep.** You can cope with just about anything if you've had enough rest, but you can cope with nothing if you haven't.

2. **Keep perspective.** All children grow up. Many of the childhood difficulties will pass. Of course, they'll be replaced by adult difficulties, but there will be plenty of time to work through those when you get there.

3. **Get informed.** Ask the parents if you can borrow a book. Understanding why your grandchild behaves the way she does will help you figure out what you should do.

4. **Simplify life.** Reduce plans for complicated outings. Make mealtime relaxed and easy. Eliminate irritants. Make as few rules as possible.

5. **Be slow to anger.** Anger and other "hot" emotions make matters worse. Find your inner peace. Develop some breathing techniques to help you stay calm in tense situations.

6. **Listen.** Your grandchild, her siblings, and her parents will all tell you important information. Be open to hearing their suggestions.

7. **Have a plan.** Knowing your strategies in advance will help you feel calm and confident. Think ahead.

8. **Be consistent.** Your grandchild appreciates routine and fears change. Keep your rules and strategies the same.

9. **Keep your sense of humor.** There will be fun times and silly times. Cherish your time together.

10. **Put guilt away.** You're going to make mistakes, but so will your grandchild. Carry on. What's important is to care and to do the best you can.

References

Dunn, W. (2009). *Living sensationally: Understanding your senses.* Philadelphia, PA: Jessica Kingsley.

Green, R. W. (2005). *The explosive child.* New York, NY: Harper Paperbacks.

Greenspan, S. I., & Wieder, S. (2006). *Engaging autism.* Cambridge, MA: Da Capo Press.

Hoopman, K. (2006). *All cats have Asperger Syndrome.* Philadelphia, PA: Jessica Kingsley.

Kranowitz, C. S. (2005). *The out-of-sync child.* New York, NY: Perigee Books.

Miller, L. J. (2007). *Sensational kids: Hope and help for children with sensory processing disorder.* New York, NY: Perigee Books.

Mucklow, N. (2009). *The sensory team handbook.* Kingston, ONT, Canada: Michael Grass House.

Mucklow, N. (2010). *Comic sense.* Kingston, ONT, Canada: Michael Grass House.

Myles, B. S., Cook, K. T., Miller, N. E., Rinner, R., & Robbins, L. A. (2000). *Asperger Syndrome and sensory issues: Practical solutions for making sense of the world.* Shawnee Mission, KS: AAPC Publishing.

Myles, B. S., & Southwick, J. (2005). *Asperger Syndrome and difficult moments: Practical solutions for tantrums, rage, and meltdowns* (rev. ed.). Shawnee Mission, KS: AAPC Publishing.

Recommended Resources

Autism Spectrum Support

Asperger Services Australia: *http://www.asperger.asn.au/*

- Asperger Syndrome Support Network Victoria Inc. (ASSNVic): *http://www.assnvic.org.au/*

- Asperger's Syndrome Support Network Qld Inc: *http://www.asperger-qld.websyte.com.au/*

- Autism and Aspergers Support Group Sydney Inc: http://www.autismsupport.org.au/

Asperger Syndrome Support Groups (UK): *http://www.aspergersupport.org.uk/support/aspergergroups.html*

Asperger Syndrome Education Network (US): *http://www.aspennj.org/resources_other.asp*

Autism Society (US): *http://www.autism-society.org/*

Autism Society of Canada: *www.autismsocietycanada.ca*

OASIS @ MAAP: *www.aspergersyndrome.org*

Grandparenting

Foundation for Grandparenting: *http://www.grandparenting.org/*

Grandparents.com: *www.grandparents.com*

Grandparents Association: *http://www.grandparents-association.org.uk/*

Grandparenting Information and Tips, from ThirdAge.com: *http://www.thirdage.com/grandparenting*

Grandparenting and Autism Spectrum Disorders

Asperger Syndrome and High Functioning Autism Association of New York (AHA-NY): *http://www.ahany.org/sg_oth.htm*

Autism Project of Rhode Island: *www.theautismproject.org/parents*

Barber National Institute: Grandparent Autism Support Group: *http://www.barberinstitute.org/prog_serv/fcss/grandparent-Support.php*

Grandparents Can Make a Difference; Autism Speaks: *http://www.autismspeaks.org/family-services/community-connections/grandparents-can-make-difference*

A Grandparent's Guide to Autism; Autism Speaks: *http://www.autismspeaks.org/family-services/community-connections/celebrating-grandparents*

Southeast Autism Research and Resource Center (SARRC): *http://www.autismcenter.org/resources.aspx*

Books to Share and Enjoy With Your Grandchildren of All Ages

Amazingly ... Alphie! Understanding and Accepting Different Ways of Being

Written for children ages 8 and up, this book fosters tolerance and acceptance while celebrating differences. The brightly illustrated book introduces readers to Alphie, a computer that is "wired differently" and has trouble fitting in and performing successfully in the world around him. After beginning to doubt his self-worth and his ability to do anything right, Alphie finally meets a human, Chris, who has been hired to fix the malfunctioning computers in the lab. Chris' patient and accepting approach totally changes Alphie's life when Alphie starts to realize that being different is what makes him special.

Suggested Age Range: 8 years and up.

ISBN 9781931282536

Roz Espin; illustrated by Beverley Ransom

Code 9927   **Price: $15.95**

A Is for Autism, F Is for Friend

A Is for Autism, F Is for Friend provides a discussion-oriented format for teaching youth about autism. In this book, Chelsea, a young girl who has severe autism, walks us through her day, including trips to the playground and park. In sharing some of her behaviors and challenges, Chelsea compares them with issues that all kids face, such as playing at recess. By demystifying her autism, she underscores the many things she and her schoolmates have in common, thus prompting a typical child to think, "Hey, I experience that, too!"

Suggested Age Range: 6-12 years.

ISBN 9781931282437

Joanna Keating-Velasco

Code 9984   **Price: $10.95**

Jackson Whole Wyoming

His classmates have identified him as a "friend" of Jackson, who has Asperger Syndrome, and now Tyler is tormented by what that means in terms of his own personality. Over the course of this highly readable and swift-moving novel, Tyler resolves this issue and in the process recalls incidents from previous school years, growing in his understanding of this unusual classmate. Great for kids in second through sixth grade.

Suggested Age Range: 6-12 years.

ISBN 9781931282727

Joan Clark

Code 9945   **Price: $16.00**

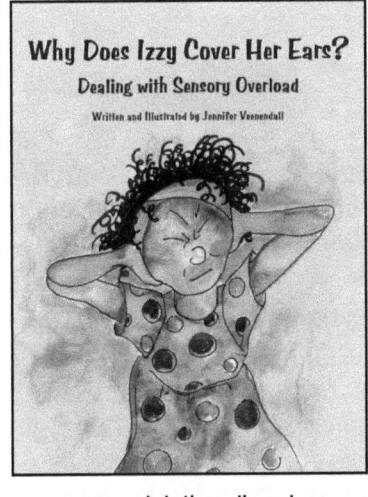

Why Does Izzy Cover Her Ears? Dealing with Sensory Overload

Meet Izzy, a feisty first grader, whose behavior is often misunderstood as she tries to cope with sensory overload in her new surroundings. This brightly illustrated book creates an environment that is accepting of students with sensory modulation difficulties, including many on the autism spectrum. It's a great resource for occupational therapists, teachers, and parents to share with children. Resources for adults at the end of the book include definitions of sensory processing and sensory modulation disorder, suggested discussion questions and lists of related books and web sites.

Suggested Age Range: 6-10 years.

ISBN 9781934575468

Written and illustrated by Jennifer Veenendall

Code 9037   **Price: $18.95**

Arnie and His School Tools: Simple Sensory Solutions That Build Success

This illustrated children's book centers around an exuberant boy who had difficulty paying attention in class and doing his schoolwork until he was equipped with tools that helped accommodate his sensory needs. The book uses simple language to describe some of the sensory tools and strategies Arnie uses at school and at home to help him achieve a more optimal level of alertness and performance. Additional resources are provided at the end of the book, including definitions of sensory processing and sensory modulation disorder, suggested discussion questions and lists of related books and websites.

Suggested Age Range: 6-10 years.

ISBN 9781934575154

Jennifer Veenendall

Code 9002   **Price: $18.95**

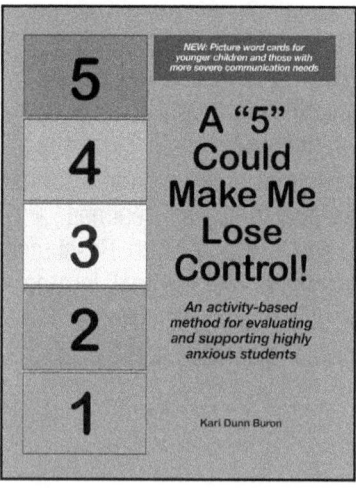

A "5" Could Make Me Lose Control! An activity-based method for evaluating and supporting highly anxious students

A "5" Could Make Me Lose Control! helps students who are highly anxious cope with their stress by classifying social and emotional information and analyzing how best to act. Using this interactive process, the student places cards that list highly stressful situations into colorful pockets designating stress levels, ranging from 5 to 1. Picture word cards make the activity suitable for students with communication challenges.

Suggested Age Range: 6-14 years.

ISBN 9781931282314

Kari Dunn Buron, MS

Code 9979   **Price: $24.95**

Ann Drew Jackson

Joan Clark's sequel to her popular book, *Jackson Whole Wyoming*, reintroduces us to Jackson Thomas, a fifth-grade boy with Asperger Syndrome. We find Jackson in a new school, with new classmates. Hillary Branson, Jackson's spunky science project partner, tells the story from her perspective. Hillary has a serious attitude problem and tends to lie; therefore, it comes as no surprise that when assigned to work with Jackson, she rebels in any way she can. As the story unfolds, the reader begins to delight in how she and Jackson discover they have a lot more in common than they ever realized.

Suggested Age Range: 10-14 years.

ISBN 9781931282451

Joan Clark

Code 9993   **Price: $17.95**

In His Shoes – A Short Journey Through Autism

In His Shoes introduces readers to Nicholas, a 13-year-old boy who has severe autism. As readers join Nicholas during his transition from elementary to middle school, they share his challenges and celebrate his successes both at home and at school. A series of "Points to Ponder" at the end of each chapter optimizes youth-friendly discussions.

Suggested Age Range: 11-15 years.

ISBN 9781934575260

Joanna Keating-Velasco

Code 9013   **Price: $18.95**

Diary of a Social Detective – Real-Life Tales of Mystery, Intrigue and Interpersonal Adventure

Diary of a Social Detective is foremost a detective/mystery story for readers ages eight and older, this book delivers insights, tools and solutions in an engaging storyline that kids can relate to. It is recommended not just for individual kids needing social skills tools, but on a broader basis for all kids wanting to read something interesting and fun. With titles such as Too Close for Comfort: The Case of Back-Away Bobby, Accidentally Funny: The Case of the Incidental Straightman, Summer's Bummer: The Case of the Huffy Girlfriends, Drowning in the Details: The Case of Monologuing Mona, etc., cleverly developed chapters allow readers to use their own social detective skills to solve the mysteries.

Suggested Age Range: 8-16 years.

ISBN 9781934575710

Jeffrey E. Jessum, PhD
Code 9063   **Price: $19.95**

My Strange and Terrible Malady

My Strange and Terrible Malady takes a look at Asperger Syndrome from Ronnie's point of view. With school already a struggle, doctors have just diagnosed 11th-grader Ronnie with Asperger Syndrome. Clearly not socially savvy, things begin to change when she meets Hannah, a fellow student who explains the mysteries of social interaction and other puzzles of daily life to Ronnie. With the help of Hannah, Ronnie shows that successful social and emotional interaction can be learned.

Suggested Age Range: 14-18 years.

ISBN 9781934575192

Catherine Bristow
Code 9011 (Book)   **Price: $15.95**
Code 9731 (Audio Book) ISBN 9781934575451   **Price: $14.95**

Herb Heiman
Code 9972

Running on Dreams

Put yourself in Brad's shoes. You're the school track star and all-around "cool guy," and you get assigned to be the "buddy" of Justin, a 15-year-old boy with autism who is starting his first semester in a mainstream school. Thrown together in a story of teenage angst, confusion and friendship, Justin and Brad share their individual perspectives as an adolescent with autism and a neurotypical teen struggling to understand each other and themselves.

Suggested Age Range: 11-18 years.

ISBN 9781931282284

Price: $18.95

Haley Morgan Myles
Code 9917

Practical Solutions to Everyday Challenges for Children with Asperger Syndrome

In this illustrated book, young author Haley Myles gives simple, no-nonsense advice on how to handle everyday occurrences that can be challenging for children and youth with Asperger Syndrome. Myles covers a range of topics, including what to do when you get a gift you don't like, if you find something that isn't yours, if you are afraid of thunderstorms and more.

Suggested Age Range: 6-12 years.

ISBN 9781931282154

Price: $14.95

Sue Diamond, MA, CCC

Code 9067

Social Rules for Kids – The Top 100 Social Rules Kids Need to Succeed

Social Rules for Kids helps open the door of communication between parent and child by addressing 100 social rules for home, school and the community. Written directly to the student, these clear rules cover topics such as body language, manners and feelings. Reminders of appropriate social rules at the end of each page are combined into a complete list at the end of the book for easy reference.

Suggested Age Range: 6-18 years.

ISBN 9781934575840

Price: $19.95

6448 Vista Dr.
Shawnee, KS 66218
www.aapcpublishing.net